Food Storage Made Easy

A Practical Approach

Sam Spencer

ISBN 13: 978-1-938091-39-1

www.samspencer.us

foodstorage@samspencer.us

INDEX

Introduction

This will be the most unique book on food storage ever written; yet it will be very complete and quite simple. We will cover many simple options for preparedness mainly in the area of food. This will be short and straight to the point and yes, *Food Storage Made Easy*.

First let's talk about food! Cooking with emergency and long-term food storage is not as difficult as it has been made out to be. This book is loaded with quick and practical methods to make it even easier. If we are talking about preparedness then we need to lay aside gourmet and focus on survival. This is not wilderness survival but survival as if there had limited resources. We need to be sure we know how to prepare simple foods. This should include having the facilities and tools to prepare those foods properly with ease and efficiency. When we talk about food storage we will also need to cover ways to prepare food including the equipment as well as the product. In this book we will build your complete *Preparedness Pantry*.

We must begin with the end in mind. First you must imagine that you are using your emergency preparedness pantry for an extended period of time. This could be due to a natural calamity or a manmade disaster. It could be due to an extended period of unemployment or illness. No matter what the reason let us first start by determining the overall needs.

As far as your preparedness pantry is concerned, if we are talking about a year's supply of food then that would simply be defined as:

365 days worth of breakfasts
365 days worth of lunches
365 days worth of dinners

If you live in a small apartment, if you are limited on space or if you are just getting starting on a tight budget then your goal might be adjusted to a ninety day supply of emergency rations, then that would be defined as:

90 days worth of breakfasts
90 days worth of lunches
90 days worth of dinners

You may want to add to that list snacks and condiments, feel free to do so as you progress. Also, if you are talking about survival and want adequate rations then you may need to skip the fancy and for that matter even eliminate over eating! We will not spend much time on medications, however you would do well to always have a 90+ day supply of medications on hand whenever possible. You should talk to your physician about this.

Let's start with breakfast. What is a typical breakfast? Maybe cereal and milk? Possibly eggs, milk and toast? Or you may be one of those people who are healthy eaters, eating such things like oatmeal or cracked wheat. Actually if you think about it, most pastries, breads, cereal and other breakfast dishes are made of basically the same ingredients but with varied portions: eggs, milk, sweetener (sugar, honey, etc.), and grain (typically in some form of flour). When you comprehend this piece of information you then can begin to plan a more complete preparedness menu where you can store and rotate the appropriate ingredients.

I am going to introduce you to several breakfast choices that you can easily prepare and sample today. You should next determine if that particular breakfast item would become one of your menu choices for your preparedness pantry menus. Once you determine the menu choices than you simply extend the volumes needed. These results will become your storage inventory. (See Appendix C) All of the recipes from which you will chose are simple and easy to prepare and designed for the use of the foods in your preparedness pantry. Preparedness pantry items should be easy to store, easy to acquire and easy to prepare.

Your emergency preparedness plan will never be complete, no matter how good it is, you will always be improving it. However there is a point where your plan is practical, functional and well established. At this point it could actually sustain you for the desired amount of time and *that should be your first goal.*

This book includes many recipes that can be easily prepared from long-term storage. Try them out and then you need to decide which recipes you will ultimately use. This leads to the next step; determining how many meals you would like to store in your long-term storage of that particular recipe.

Once you get the feel for this system introduce your own recipes to your plan then add the product totals to your preparedness program.

Now let's have some fun!

Before We Get Started

Your preparedness pantry plan should include water storage. The bare minimum of water that a person needs is 1 gallon per day. This gives you up to 3 quarts for drinking and then 1 quart for cooking. I round this off to one 55-gallon drum of water for 2 people per month. Since most of your cooking needs require water it is even more important to store some water.

An easy way to do this is to rinse out 2-liter pop bottles, fill them with water and store them somewhere out-of-the-way. You can also purchase larger containers that are excellent for storing water. We will not go more into water, there is a lot said that you could easily get a hold of.

Another important thing to consider is balanced nutrition. You need to be sure that you have grains, vegetables, fruit, and dairy in your diet. Most of the recipes you will find in this book lead to a balance diet. In other words, you can't just eat wheat! You need a balanced diet!

Also the longevity of the items in your preparedness pantry can vary. For example: most canned products will last between 1 to 2 years. Most dried and powdered products can last 10 or more years. If you bottle your own fruits and vegetables correctly they can last 5 to 10 years without a problem. Nevertheless the best idea of all is to eat on a regular basis those fruits and vegetables which you bottle yourself. If you subscribe to the philosophy that you will *bottle what you use then use what you bottle* you will find greater success. Rotate your foods where needed. It is also very important to use food from your preparedness pantry regularly.

Breakfast Menus

The first step is to determine what you WILL eat. Just having a big supply of food storage could be frustrating when you find out that you have forgotten to store an essential ingredient or that you have no idea how to use nor how to prepare what you have stored on a whim. It is for this reason that you start with the end in mind. If you know exactly what you are going to eat then you will be more likely to have what you need when you need it. The easier to forget items such as baking soda or baking powder will then be adequately stored and in the needed amounts.

You will notice that many of the basic recipes contain wheat, oil, liquid, a leavening agent and sweetener. The eggs and fruit are bonuses. A wheat grinder is not necessary to use your storage wheat. A good blender will do in most cases. In an emergency you will find that the easy to make blender pancake recipe will provide all one needs with very little effort. They can be made with all powdered ingredients such as; powdered eggs, powdered milk and powdered shortening. You just add the appropriate amount of water. The recipes in this book are easy to prepare, tasty and fit perfectly into our long-term preparedness pantry program.

Once you have decided on the recipes that you will incorporate in your preparedness menu the next step is logical and easy. How much will you want to have in reserve for your family? Remember that you want 365 days worth of breakfasts, lunches and dinners.

Here is an example:

Assume you want to have in storage 100 preparations of the *Blender Pancakes, Dry Ingredients* recipe. That means that of the 365 days worth of breakfasts that you plan to store, these calculations will include the ingredients for 100 family meals, leaving you 265 additional meal preparations that you must also store. Keep in mind that this recipe will feed a family of three or four people. You will need to adjust the recipe for the number of people for whom you are maintaining preparations. In other words, if there are six or seven in your family you should double everything. In this example we will assume a family of four.

Blender Pancake Dry Ingredients:

1 C. wheat berries/kernels

3 Tbls. powdered milk

2 Tbls. powdered butter, margarine or shortening

2 Tbls. powdered eggs

2 tsps. baking powder

3 Tbls. brown sugar or honey

1/2 tsp. salt

You will need to take each ingredient and multiply by 100 to arrive at the total quantity you will need to maintain for this preparation in your preparedness pantry.

Below are the calculations for what you will need to store for this recipe at 100 preparations for a family of four:

- **100 cups** of Wheat berries/kernels (total wheat) ÷ **16** (cups in a gallon) = *6 1/4 gallons of wheat* for pancakes.
- **300 Tablespoons** of powdered milk (total powdered milk) ÷ **16** (tablespoon in a cup) = *18 3/4 cups of powdered milk*. (A number 10 can will hold about 12 cups. With these figures you will need two #10 cans of powdered milk to have this particular need met.)
- **200 Tablespoons** of powdered butter, margarine or shortening (total powdered butter) ÷ **16** (Tablespoon in a cup) = *12 1/2 cups of powdered butter, margarine or shortening*.
- **200 Tablespoons** of powdered eggs (total powdered eggs) ÷ **16** (tablespoon in a cup) = *12 1/2 cups of powdered eggs*.
- **200 teaspoons** baking powder (total baking powder) ÷ **48** (teaspoon in a cup) = *4.2 cups of baking powder*.
- **300 Tablespoons** of powdered sugar (total powdered sugar) ÷ **16** (tablespoon in a cup) = *18 3/4 cups of brown sugar*.
- **50 teaspoons** salt (total salt) ÷ **48** (teaspoon in a cup) = *1.1 cups of salt*.

Now just add these totals to the totals in you long-term preparedness pantry program. Do this with each recipe you plan to put in your emergency preparedness pantry cookbook and you will know exactly *what* you need to store and *how much* of each item.

The totals for this example will be:

> 6 1/4 gallons of wheat
>
> 18 3/4 cups of powdered milk
>
> 12 1/2 cups of powdered butter, margarine or shortening
>
> 12 1/2 cups of powdered eggs
>
> 4.2 cups of baking powder
>
> 18 3/4 cups of brown sugar
>
> 1.1 cups of salt

See Appendix E for Universal Volume Calculation Table

Remember that this is only 100 days worth of breakfasts, or about 30% of your breakfast needs. There are 265 more breakfasts to plan!

Now review each recipe. Cook a sample so you will know how to use and prepare this preparedness pantry recipe and most importantly you will know exactly what your family *will* eat. This may seem like a lot of work but it will be worth the trouble once you develop a preparedness pantry plan that is based on what you *know* how to prepare plus you are now storing what you *will* use.

So in a nutshell, plan your menus and then store enough to feed your family those meals for a year. Yes, it is that simple, it just takes a

little time to plan and figure the needed quantities. Ultimately you will come up with an inventory list that is accurate, that will be your guide on quantities to maintain in your preparedness pantry.

Once you have determined the needs for your 365 breakfast preparations then you follow the same plan for lunch and dinner. You can also plan snacks and deserts, but first finish the three basic meals and then you can move on to the luxuries. Luxuries can always be added later, however a few words of advice:

Never add anything to your preparedness pantry without knowing *why you are adding it and how to use it!*

If all of this seems to be a little too much and you prefer boxes of dry cereal that's okay. You just need to be sure that you have enough boxes and that you rotate your boxes.

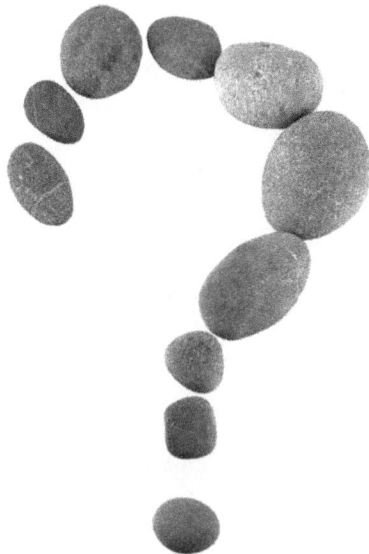

Taking The First Step

Start with the end in mind!

Build a functional "Preparedness Pantry"

The first step is to try the recipes that are listed in this book, and then you will know what it is you need to stock in your preparedness pantry.

Steps That You Will Follow:

1. Choose the recipes for your emergency storage meals.

2. Cook a sample to determine what you *will* eat.

3. Determine how many preparations you would like.

4. Extend the ingredients needed for preparations.

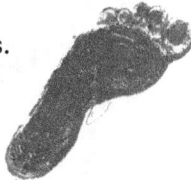

5. Total the extended amounts for storage quantities.

6. Work toward acquiring those quantities.

BREAKFASTS

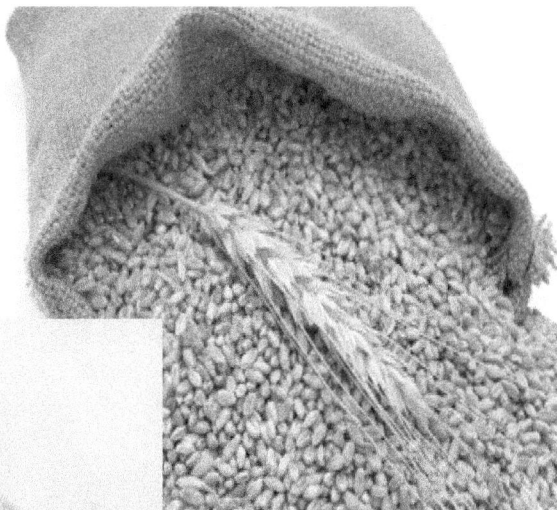

Pancakes

Pancakes are fast and easy to prepare. They are an ideal long-term preparedness pantry item and for that matter these pancakes can be a preparation that can be used in your everyday menus.

Pancakes are universal! Spread on some peanut butter then add a little jelly and you have a peanut butter and jelly sandwich. Wrap it around a hotdog with some mustard and relish and that's a great dinner. Cook a few extra and then save them for snacks, freeze them for another meal and then warm them in the microwave. Add banana and nuts for banana-nut pancakes that can double as Banana Nut bread. Put some pancakes in a plastic bag in the fridge and they will disappear quickly.

The following recipes are a few variations on pancakes that can be made from long-term preparedness pantry items. Try them all and choose your favorites. Experiment and make your own variations. This is an easy way to introduce to your family preparedness pantry cooking!

Preparedness Pantry Substitutions To Keep In Mind

- Oil = Equal amount of Applesauce
- 1 Egg = 2 Tbsp. Powdered egg + 2 Tbsp. warm water
- 1 Cup milk = 2 Tbsp. Powdered milk + 3/4 Cup warm water
- 1 Cup wheat kernels = 1 1/4 Cup ground wheat flour
- Butter = One part Powdered Butter + One part water
- Margarine = One part Powdered Margarine + One part water
- Shortening = One part Powdered Shortening + One part water
- Cheese = One part Powdered Cheese + Two parts water
- Sour Cream = One part powdered Sour Cream + One part water

(See Appendix E)

The use of powdered products in the production of foods is widely used commercially today. They make an excellent long-term storage resource. They will last many years and can largely be used interchangeably. Begin to work with powdered ingredients in your daily cooking and you will be way ahead of the curve when you have to dip into your preparedness pantry.

As you go through this book keep this page in mind, begin to see yourself using powdered products regularly.

Conversions:

Divide Total teaspoons by 48 to convert to Cups

Divide Total Tablespoons by 16 to convert to Cups

Divide Total Cups by 16 to convert to Gallons

Blender Whole Wheat Pancakes
MAKES: 12 – 5" pancakes

1 cup whole wheat kernel in blender or (1 1/4 cups whole wheat flour)

1 1/3 cups milk

1/4 cup vegetable oil

1 egg

2 teaspoons baking powder

3 Tbls. brown sugar

1/2 teaspoon salt

Directions:

Blend milk with wheat for 5 minutes.

Add the rest of the ingredients and blend 2 additional minutes.

Cook on a hot skillet until done.

Use quickly so the cracked wheat stays suspended in batter.

Variations:

Replace the oil with 1/3 C of applesauce or peaches; you should also use less sugar (1 ½ - 2T).

Blender Pancakes are one of the easiest breakfasts you can make from your preparedness pantry, just add a little fruit to make it the prefect breakfast!

Blender Whole Wheat Pancakes
Made From All Dried Ingredients
MAKES: 12 –18 5" pancakes

Dry Ingredients

1 C. wheat berries/kernels in blender or (1 1/4 cups whole wheat flour)

3 Tablespoon powdered milk

2 Tbls. or powdered butter, margarine, or shortening

2 Tbls. powdered eggs

2 teaspoons baking powder

3 Tbls. brown sugar or honey

1/2 teaspoon salt

Wet Ingredients

2 cups warm water (warm to hot water for easier mixing of dried dairy products)

Directions:

Blend water with wheat for 5 minutes.

Add the rest of the ingredients and blend 2 additional minutes.

Cook on a hot skillet until done.

Use immediately so the cracked wheat stays suspended in batter.

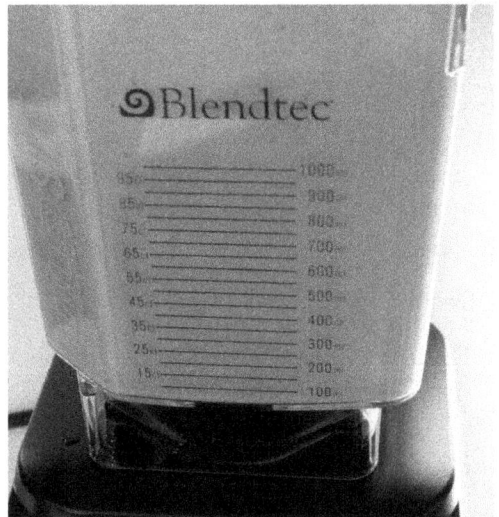

Banana Nut Whole Wheat Pancakes
MAKES: 12 – 5" pancakes

1 cup whole wheat kernels in blender or (1 1/4 cups whole wheat flour)

1 Tablespoon brown sugar (note less sugar)

2 teaspoons baking powder

1/4 teaspoon salt

1 1/4 cups milk

1 egg

1/4 cup oil

1/4 cup chopped pecans

1/2 cup Overripe Banana

(one medium banana)

Directions

- Blend water with wheat for 5 minutes.
- Add the rest of the ingredients and blend 2 additional minutes.
- Fold in chopped pecans.
- Pour onto lightly greased hot griddle; turn when bubbles form on top of pancakes. Cook until second side is golden brown
- Use dried bananas - soak 1/2 Cup dried bananas in water to reconstitute.

If you like banana nut bread you will love this pancake. Serve it with a little whip cream on top of sliced peaches or other fruit.

TIP:

Mix dry ingredients and place into re-sealable bags until ready for use. Add 1 part warm water to 1 part dry mix to make as many or as few as you like. Double, triple or even many more times the recipe to always have healthy "just add water" pancake mix.

One may ask, what if I don't have a blender? This problem can easily be solved with a small 2000 watt generator. You can then run your generator for the 7 to 10 min. required to prepare your pancake mix. You could also use your generator to power an electric griddle. This generator is efficient and will run close to 8 hours on a gallon of gasoline.

"The Kitchen Mill" from Blendtec is a great mill that can handle almost all grains with excellent results. This amazing mill can be purchased for less than $200. A must for every preparedness pantry! The above mentioned generator will also save you with this appliance!

You should also consider some manual way to grind your wheat into flour. The Victorio VKP1024 Deluxe Hand Operated Grain Mill as pictured here can be purchased for less than $100 and is ideal for hand grinding.

This mill will grind corn and other grains plus it makes excellent cracked wheat when the grinding wheels are backed off.

Photo Courtesy
www.victorio.info

MUFFINS

Make one of these quick and easy breakfast treats, muffins! A muffin and a breakfast drink is a staple for many commuters in a hurry. You can learn to make amazing muffins from your preparedness pantry from scratch using these muffin recipes. I caution you however, you may like them so much that you could choose to make them on a regular basis, not just for emergency cooking.

Blender Muffins

You can put the wheat kernels right into the blender with the liquid, turn it on high and blend for five full minutes. Then add the balance of the ingredients and blend for an additional two minutes and your batter is now smooth and ready. Use quickly so the suspended particles do not settle to the bottom. Follow the same recipe with milled flour either in the blender or the mixer, blend until smooth.

Whole Wheat Banana Muffins
Servings: 12 -16

2 very ripe large bananas

1/3 cup vegetable oil

1 Egg

1 1/2 cup soy or 2% milk

1 1/2 cups whole wheat

Or (1 1/4 cups wheat berries/kernels)

1/2 tsp. salt

2 tsps. Baking powder

1/3 cup loosely packed brown sugar or 1/4 cup honey

Directions:

1. Preheat oven to 350^0 and grease or line with paper muffin tin

2. Blend milk, bananas, egg and oil in blender

3. Add wheat, grind in blender (2-3 minutes)

4. Add salt, baking powder and brown sugar

5. Mix until batter is smooth

6. Add chopped, raisins, chocolate chips or other treats as desired

7. Pour the batter into greased muffin tin and bake at 350^0 for approximately 25 - 30 minutes, until lightly brown and firm to touch.

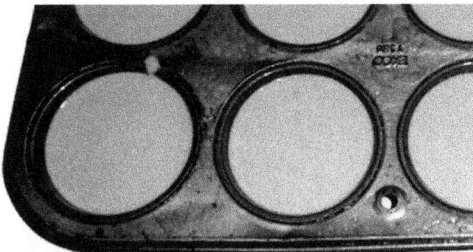

The batter should be about 1/4" below the top of pan.

Whole Wheat Banana Muffins
From Dried Ingredients
Servings: 12 – 16

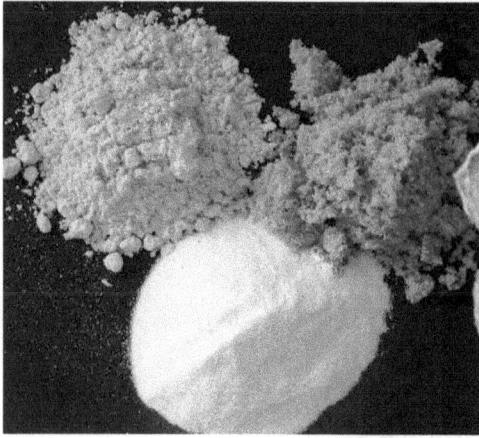

You will use all dried ingredients with this recipe. This can be an excellent preparedness pantry recipe. It can easily be prepared and cooked almost anywhere with limited resources. You can plan and store this preparation today and it will still be ready in five plus years!

Ingredients:

1/2 Cup dried bananas (soak in the water from recipe to soften)

2 Cups Water

1/3 Cup Powdered shortening

2 Tbsp. Powdered Eggs

3 Tbsp. Powdered milk

1 1/2 cups whole wheat or (1 1/4 cups whole wheat berries/kernels)

1/2 tsp. salt

2 tsps. Baking powder

1/3 cup loosely packed brown sugar or 1/4 cup honey

Directions:

1. Preheat oven to 350^0 and grease or line with paper muffin tin

2. Blend water, bananas, egg and oil in blender

3. Add wheat, grind in blender (5 minutes)

4. Add salt, baking powder and brown sugar

5. Mix until batter is smooth

6. Fold in nuts, and raisins if desired

7. Pour the batter into greased muffin tin and bake at 350^0 for approximately 25 - 30 minutes, until lightly brown and firm to touch.

TIP:

It is a good idea to learn how to use powdered ingredients in your meal planning. Powders are excellent in baking and have a very long storage life. Powders can be the answer to storage questions such as milk, butter, cheese and shortening just to name few. Contact your local supplier and ask about powders. (See Appendix E)

Whole Wheat Chocolate Banana Muffins
Servings: 12 - 16

Ingredients:

2 very ripe large bananas

1/3 cup vegetable oil

1 Egg

1 1/2 cup water

1 1/2 cups whole wheat

or (1 1/4 cups whole

wheat berries/kernels)

2 packets of instant hot coco drink mix

or 1/3 Cup of powdered chocolate milk mix (3 envelopes for chocoholics)

1/2 tsp. salt

2 tsps. Baking powder

1/3 cup loosely packed brown sugar or 1/4 cup honey

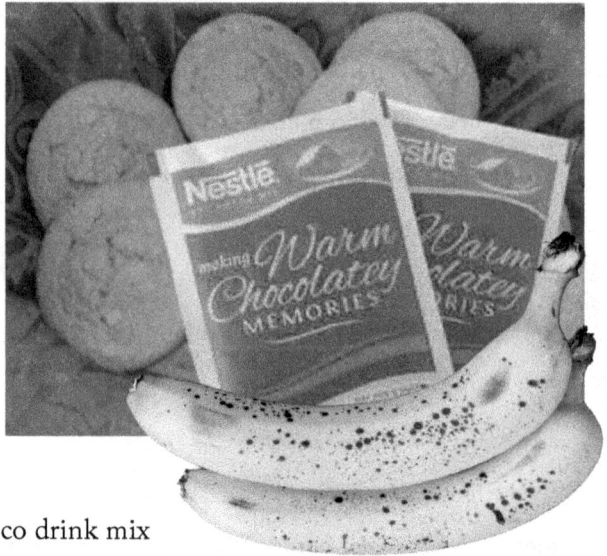

Directions:

1. Preheat oven to 350^0 and grease or line with paper muffin tins

2. Blend milk, bananas, egg and oil in blender

3. Add wheat, grind in blender (5 minutes min)

4. Add salt, baking powder, coco mix and brown sugar

5. Mix until batter is smooth. You may stir in chocolate chips if desired before pouring into muffin tins.

6. Pour the batter into greased muffin tin and bake at 350^0 for approximately 25 - 30 minutes, until lightly brown and firm to touch.

Whole Wheat Applesauce Muffins
Servings: 12 - 16

1 1/2 cups whole wheat or (1 1/4 cups whole wheat berries/kernels)

3/4 Cup Applesauce (1/2 can applesauce)

1 1/2 cups milk

1 Egg

1/3 cup brown sugar

1/2 tsp. salt

2 tsps. Baking powder

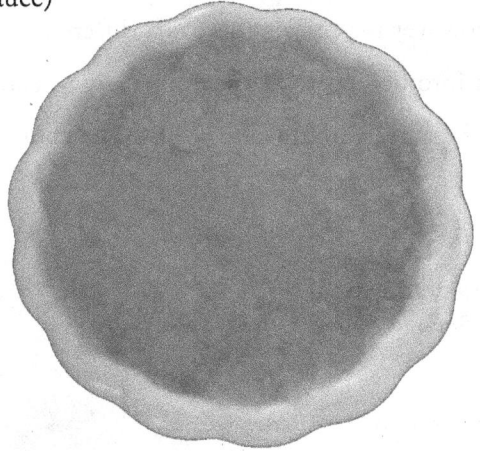

Directions:

1. Preheat oven to 350^0 and grease or line with paper muffin tins
2. Blend milk, applesauce, and egg in blender
3. Add wheat, grind in blender (5 minutes min)
4. Add salt, baking powder and brown sugar
5. Mix until batter is smooth
6. Pour the batter into greased muffin tin and bake at 350^0 for approximately 25 - 30 minutes, until lightly brown and firm to touch.

NOTE:

Your blender must have at least 450 watts. Do not double the recipe in your blender, you must make additional batches.

TIP:

* *Put an orange peel in your hard brown sugar and in the morning it will be soft again.*
* *Some people think the taste of whole wheat is too strong, if so add a few drops of vanilla.*

Oatmeal

Two types of oatmeal are great for the preparedness pantry, the instant oatmeal and the three-minute style. For baking they are interchangeable, however for cereals there is a difference. The instant is instant, you can pour it into boiling milk and it is ready to eat, no more cooking, no more waiting. The three-minute oats needs to be cooked and will be a bit mushier and there are many who love it that way.

Easy Oatmeal
1 Serving

Ingredients:

1/2 cup milk

1/2 cup of instant oatmeal

Add extras as desired:

1/2 – 1 t. Cinnamon

1 Tbsp. Brown sugar as desired

1/4 Cup Raisins

1/4 Cup Chopped dried apples

Directions:

Add the extras you desire to the milk.

Bring milk to a boil in the microwave.

Stir in the instant oatmeal; stir it in until you reach the consistency you like. You can replace milk with powdered milk as follows: 1 Tbsp. of powder to each 1/2 cup of water.

Three-Minute Oatmeal

Three-minute oatmeal is cooked for three minutes, which is of course why it is called three-minute oatmeal.

Three-Minute Oatmeal
1 Serving

Ingredients:

1/2 cup milk

1/2 cup of three-minute oatmeal

Add extras as desired:

1 Tbsp. Brown sugar as desired

1/2 – 1 t. Cinnamon

1/4 Cup Raisins

1/4 Cup Chopped dried apples

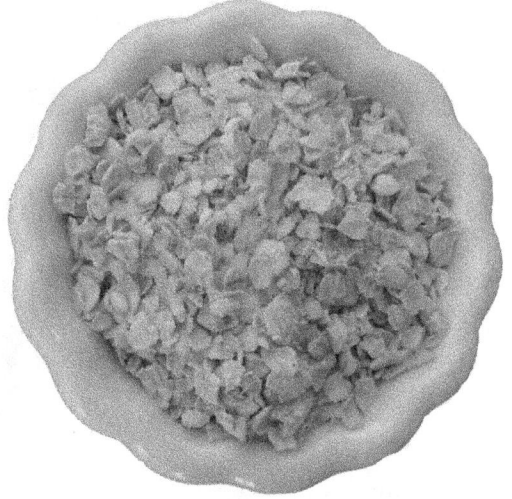

Directions:

- Add the extras you desire to the milk.
- Bring milk to a boil in the microwave.
- Stir in the oatmeal; stir it in until you reach the consistency you like.
- Bring you liquid to a boil, turn down the heat and stir in all ingredients. Stir as the oatmeal cooks. Remove from heat and let it cool. EASY!

That is it! If you like oatmeal you will love this easy way to make oatmeal.

Cracked Wheat

Serves 4

To make one cup of cracked wheat:

1 cup cracked wheat (can be cracked in a mill or a blender)

2 cups water

3 - 6 Tbsp. brown sugar (It's the molasses in the brown sugar is what makes it so good)

1 pat of butter (optional)

1/4 tsp. salt (optional)

4 Tbsp. Powdered milk (optional)

Directions:

1. In a small saucepan bring water to a boil.
2. Stir in all ingredients.
3. Stir for about one minute to mix milk in well.
4. Turn down heat to low and stir as needed to keep from burning. Cover with lid, but stir often. This may take 5 to 10 minutes.
5. The wheat is done when soft and creamy, you will cook the wheat too your taste.

To crack wheat in the blender please see instruction on page 30.

Four Serving Calculations

Easy Oatmeal
4 Serving

Ingredients:

2 cups milk or 4 Tbls. of powdered milk and 1 3/4 cups water

2 cups of instant oatmeal

Three-Minute Oatmeal
4 Serving

Ingredients:

2 cups milk or 4 Tbls. of powdered milk and 1 3/4 cups water

2 cups of instant oatmeal

Add extras as desired:

1/2 – 1 t. Cinnamon

1 Tbsp. Brown sugar as desired

1/4 Cup Raisins

1/4 Cup Chopped dried apples

50 Preparations for a family of four:

200 Tbls. of powdered milk = 12.5 cups

100 cups of instant oatmeal = 6.25 gallons

Don't forget to add the extras!

Make your calculations and then add the numbers to Appendix C

Thermos Method

1. Bring water to a hard boil.

2. Pour water into thermos

3. Quickly stir in all ingredients

4. Seal and let sit overnight

This should be ready to eat in the morning. A good glass thermos should keep the water hot enough to cook and hydrate the wheat.

Cracking Wheat in your blender:

This is easy but a bit scary the first time largely because it is quite noisy, but it works. Put a small amount of wheat kernels (1/2 to 2/3 cup max) in your blender and pulse. Do not overload your blender. You want the kernels to become slightly chopped up. Remember that you are not making flour. Once the wheat berries/kernels are cracked stop, they are done.

Remove the cracked wheat from the blender and if you choose sift out the flour with a flour sifter or a very fine-screened strainer. You can add this flour to bread, pancakes or muffins. If you do not remove the flour that is perfectly fine, your cracked wheat will be a little bit on the mushy side because of the fine flour but that may be your preference.

Whole Kernel Wheat
Makes 2 servings

Thermos Wheat

Thermos wheat is the name I give whole kernel wheat soaked overnight in boiling hot water. Here is how to make thermos wheat:

1 cup whole wheat kernels

2 cups boiling water

1/2 teaspoon salt

- It is good idea to preheat a thermos by filling it with hot tap water then empty the thermos before you add the boiling water.
- Bring 2 cups of water to a boil and add salt then pour the wheat in the thermos and add the boiling water.
- Seal the thermos and shake to surrounded all kernels by water
- Let the wheat cook for about 8 - 10 hours (overnight).
- Drain water and serve with milk, sugar or raisins.

This is a very simple but healthy breakfast preparation with just five minutes of work the night before. To add more nutrition sprout the wheat before you put it in boiling water and cook overnight. Sprouting your wheat before you cook it will multiply many times the nutritional value of wheat and it becomes more easily assimilated and useable by the body.

How To Sprout Your Wheat:

1. Put 1/2 cup of wheat berries/kernels into a jar with 1 cup water. (Use this ratio to sprout more or less)
2. Let the wheat soak for 10 - 12 hours this will give the wheat ample time to swell.

3. Drain the water and rinse the wheat several times.
4. Leave the wheat in the jar another 12 hours.
5. Repeat steps 3 and 4 two more times
6. Wheat is now ready to eat!

When the sprout is between 1/4 and the length if the kernel it is ready.

Sprouting is simple and a great way to add additional nutrition. Don't be afraid to use sprouts! Try adding sprouts to your pancakes, muffins and breads. They can be added to salads to give a nutty texture enhancing flavor plus added nutrition. Add sprouts to your salads for a new look and taste. You will find that a little goes a long way!

For more on general sprouting see section on sprouting page 111.

Crockpot Wheat

Crockpot wheat is another way to cook your whole wheat. You will use more water than thermos wheat plus you cook it in a crockpot. The extra water is because more is absorbed in the wheat and it also some boils off.

1/2 cup wheat

2 - 2 1/2 Cups water

1/2 teaspoon salt

Add butter and sugar if desired at this time.

Instructions:

Place all the ingredients into a small crockpot and let it cook until done. The length will be determined by the heating capacity of the crockpot and your personal preference. Also the water may boil all off in a hotter crockpot so in addition to time the amount of water may need to be adjusted. Any excess water can always be poured off. This method will be a little mushier than the thermos wheat as it is cooked a little more. This method can also be done overnight on low heat settings, be sure to have extra water.

TIP

You can also use sprouted wheat in the crockpot wheat for a more nutritious breakfast. To learn how to sprout wheat, refer to the section on Sprouting Wheat on the previous page.

Powdered Eggs

Learn to effectively use powdered goods. That would be primarily powdered eggs, milk, cheese, butter and others. One #10 can of egg mix is a little more than 8 dozen eggs. Powdered ingredients can be used in almost any recipe with water adjustment. (See Appendix E)

Scrambled Eggs

Scrambled eggs from powdered eggs are not as bad as it may sound, mix in a little salsa and ham and you have a scrambled omelet. If you get good at using powdered eggs you can make a regular omelet that is tasty and fresh. There is no doubt that you have had powdered eggs in a commercial setting most certainly in baking and very likely in other preparations.

For one egg you mix 2 Tbls. of powdered Eggs to 2 Tbls. of hot water. The ratio is 1 to 1 for powdered eggs. There are several kinds of egg mixes, whole egg, egg whites and egg mix. Be sure you choose the kind that is designed for scrambling. This egg mix can be used interchangeably for cooking in the same ratio of 2 Tbls. of powdered Eggs to 2 Tbls. of hot water that equals one egg.

For a family of four with 2 eggs each that would be 8 Tbls. powdered eggs per breakfast. 50 preparations would be 50 X 8 = 200 ÷ 16 = 12.5 cups.

French Toast

French toast is a breakfast you should also consider, especially when you make homemade whole-wheat bread. Use powdered eggs and milk to make the egg batter that you dip your bread into and your French toast will be excellent.

Directions:

- Mix well 1/4 cup of egg mix and 1 teaspoon of powdered milk into 1/3 cup of hot water.
- Dip your bread into the egg and milk mixture.
- Cook on a hot griddle.

This recipe will make 3-4 slices of French toast. Refer to the bread recipe in the next section to determine how much extra bread making ingredients you will need if you include French toast in your menu selection then add the totals to your preparedness pantry inventory worksheet.

TIP:

This is a good place to use your bread as it begins to lose its freshness. The egg batter will moisten the bread and make it fresh again. Do not forget to add to your preparedness pantry syrup and jams that you might use as topping.

Breakfast Menu Total Volume Table

Now it's time to bring it all together as far as breakfasts are concerned.

Enter quantities needed for each menu preparation from your choices then extend to grand TOTAL for breakfast preparedness needs

Mark "t" teaspoons, "T" Tablespoons or "C" cups above input number

#Preparations	Pancakes			Muffins			Oatmeal			Wheat									Grad Total		
Ingredients	t	T	C	t	T	C	t	T	C	t	T	C	t	T	C	t	T	C	t	T	C
Apples, Dried																					
Applesauce																					
Baking Powder																					
Baking Soda																					
Bananas, Dried																					
Butter, Powdered																					
Catsup																					
Chocolate Chips																					
Chocolate Milk																					
Cinnamon																					
Cold Cereal																					
Eggs, Powdered																					
Flour, Baking																					
Honey																					
Jam/Jelly																					

	t	T	C	t	T	C	t	T	C	t	T	C	t	T	C	t	T	C
Margarine, Powdered	t	T	C	t	T	C	t	T	C	t	T	C	t	T	C	t	T	C
Milk, Powdered	t	T	C	t	T	C	t	T	C	t	T	C	t	T	C	t	T	C
Nuts	t	T	C	t	T	C	t	T	C	t	T	C	t	T	C	t	T	C
Oatmeal, 3-minute	t	T	C	t	T	C	t	T	C	t	T	C	t	T	C	t	T	C
Oatmeal, Instant	t	T	C	t	T	C	t	T	C	t	T	C	t	T	C	t	T	C
Raisins	t	T	C	t	T	C	t	T	C	t	T	C	t	T	C	t	T	C
Salsa	t	T	C	t	T	C	t	T	C	t	T	C	t	T	C	t	T	C
Salt	t	T	C	t	T	C	t	T	C	t	T	C	t	T	C	t	T	C
Shortening/ Oil, Powdered	t	T	C	t	T	C	t	T	C	t	T	C	t	T	C	t	T	C
Sugar, Brown	t	T	C	t	T	C	t	T	C	t	T	C	t	T	C	t	T	C
Sugar, Granulated	t	T	C	t	T	C	t	T	C	t	T	C	t	T	C	t	T	C
Syrup, Maple	t	T	C	t	T	C	t	T	C	t	T	C	t	T	C	t	T	C
Wheat, Flour	t	T	C	t	T	C	t	T	C	t	T	C	t	T	C	t	T	C
Wheat, Storage	t	T	C	t	T	C	t	T	C	t	T	C	t	T	C	t	T	C
Yeast, Dried	t	T	C	t	T	C	t	T	C	t	T	C	t	T	C	t	T	C
	t	T	C	t	T	C	t	T	C	t	T	C	t	T	C	t	T	C
	t	T	C	t	T	C	t	T	C	t	T	C	t	T	C	t	T	C
	t	T	C	t	T	C	t	T	C	t	T	C	t	T	C	t	T	C
	t	T	C	t	T	C	t	T	C	t	T	C	t	T	C	t	T	C
	t	T	C	t	T	C	t	T	C	t	T	C	t	T	C	t	T	C

Recipe Calculator

Use this worksheet to help organize your recipes and extend the totals to the **Preparedness Pantry Inventory Consolidated Worksheet.**
Appendix C

____150____ Number Preparations   ___*Whole Wheat Pancakes*___   Recipe

Volume	Ingredient	# Preparations	Total Needed		Total Needed
__1__ Cups	*Wheat* X	__150__ =	__150__ ÷ 16 =	__9.375__	Gallons
__2__ Tbls	*P. Eggs* X	__150__ =	__300__ ÷ 16 =	__18.75__	Cups
__3__ Tbls	*P. Milk* X	__150__ =	__450__ ÷ 16 =	__28.125__	Cups
__3__ Tbls	*Sugar* X	__150__ =	__450__ ÷ 16 =	__28.125__	Cups
__2__ Tbls	*P. Butter* X	__150__ =	__300__ ÷ 16 =	__18.75__	Cups
__2__ tsps.	*B Powder* X	__150__ =	__300__ ÷ 48 =	__6.25__	Cups
__1/2__ tsps.	*Salt* X	__150__ =	__75__ ÷ 48 =	__1.5__	Cups

Script Indicates Your Calculations

Add total Needed to Appendix C

For additional Recipe Calculator worksheets see appendix H

Breakfast Menu Total Volume Table

Mark "t" teaspoons, "T" Tablespoons or "C" cups above input number

#Preparations	150	50	50	50	50		Grad Total
Ingredients	Pancakes	Muffins	Oatmeal	Wheat	Eggs		Grad Total
	t · T · C	t · T · C	t · T · C	t · T · C	t · T · C	t · T · C	t · T · C
Apples, Dried							
Applesauce		15 (C)					15 (C)
Baking Powder	300 (t)	100 (t)					400 (t)
Baking Soda							
Bananas, Dried		25 (C)					25 (C)
Butter, Powdered					50 (T)		50 (T)
Catsup							
Chocolate Chips							
Chocolate Milk							
Cinnamon							
Cold Cereal							
Eggs, Powdered	300 (T)	100 (T)					400 (T)
Flour, Baking							

Script Indicates Your Calculations

	t	T	c	t	T	c	t	T	c	t	T	c	t	T	c	t	T	c	t	T	c
Honey																					
Jam/Jelly																					
Margarine, Powdered																					
Milk, Powdered		600			150						100			100						950	
Nuts																					
Oatmeal, 3-minute																					
Oatmeal, Instant						100															100
Raisins					50															50	
Salsa																					
Salt	75			25															100		
Shortening/ Oil, Powdered		300				17															36
Sugar, Brown		450				17		100													52
Sugar, Granulated																					
Syrup																					
Wheat, Flour																					
Wheat, Storage			150			75						100			50						375
Yeast, Dried																					

Divide Total teaspoons by 48 to convert to Cups

Divide Total Tablespoons by 16 to convert to Cups

Divide Total Cups by 16 to convert to Gallons

It's Your Turn

It's your turn to create a few breakfast recipes. Now you know what is important. You know how to fit product into your preparedness program and daily menus.

Write down your recipes on the next few pages. Make sure that they fit the preparedness criterion:

Preparedness pantry items should be:

- Easy to store
- Easy to acquire
- Easy to prepare

Once you have written down your recipe then determine how many times in 365 days you will serve that preparation. Be sure to adjust the quantities for the size of your family.

Finally transfer the totals to the *Breakfast Menu Total Volume Table* by listing your menu by name and adding the totals to the grand total.
(See Appendix C)

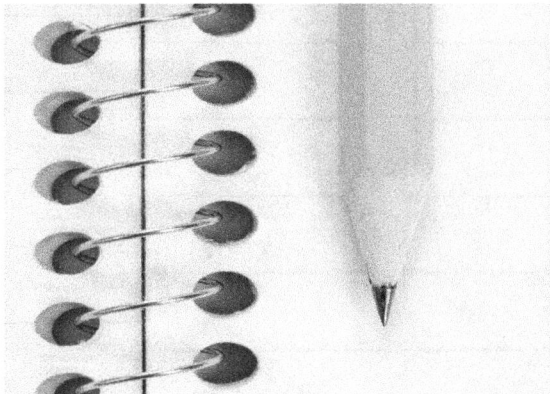

Your Recipe

Your Recipe

Your Recipe

LUNCH IDEAS AND BREADS

Lunch Ideas And Breads

Lunches are different things to different people, for some it is the largest meal of the day and for others it is a fleeting snack so they will be able to keep working. Whatever it is in any case you must have adequate storage for 365 meals. That could be as simple as 365 packages of Ramen Noodles for each individual!

There are many preparations that you can consider for a lunch menu, for example in the dried category you will find excellent soup mixes, noodles and other instant preparations.

Some other ideas to consider would be some of the canned product such as stews, soups and meats. The shelf life of canned goods is typically one to two years and these be rotated. This will be acceptable in the preparations you choose, however, canned goods absolutely must be rotated. There are excellent shelving and rotation systems that can be bought commercially to rotate canned goods. You can design whatever system you like, however, it is very important to rotate your storage items.

Let us begin with a few simple breads. There is no need to overwhelm yourself with a multitude of various recipes I recommend one bread recipe and it is universal. I also have provided a basic recipe for cornbread. Certainly you may feel free to expand on your preparedness pantry by adding recipes that are your favorites, that are easy to prepare, and for which you will be able to successfully store all items.

Lunch and dinner preparations, in many cases, may be the same. The most important thing to consider here is to define what you will eat! Once you know what you will prepare the rest is easy, simply extend the recipes.

The purpose of this book is to give you a foundation and a process to easily establish your preparedness pantry with items that you will use and in the quantities that you will need for your size family.

TIP:

Incorporate the meal selections from you preparedness pantry in your weekly menus. Set a goal to serve two breakfasts, two lunches and two dinners from your preparedness pantry each week. In doing this you will become expert with your chosen preparations and also provide for regular rotation in your preparedness pantry.

Whole Wheat Bread

Basic Whole Wheat Bread Recipe

1 3/4 cups water

4 cups whole wheat flour (Grind in mill)

2 teaspoons salt

2 Tbls. honey or brown sugar

2 Tbls. dry milk powder

2 Tbls. powdered eggs

2 Tbls. shortening or oil

2 teaspoons active dry yeast

Directions:

Place ingredients in bread machine pan in the order suggested by the manufacturer. Select appropriate setting, and then press Start.

This recipe does not need to be made in the bread machine and can be mixed by hand or just make the dough in the machine and cook separately. This will simply involve a little more work. Put it in your bread pans, let it rise and bake at 350°F for 45 minutes.

See Appendix H for sample worksheet

Whole Wheat Rolls

I use the *Basic Whole Wheat Bread Recipe* for whole wheat dinner rolls. Put the machine on the "Dough" setting and mix the dough.

Ingredients:

1 3/4 cups water

4 cups whole wheat flour (Grind in grinder)

2 teaspoons salt

1/3 cup honey or brown sugar

2 Tbls. dry milk powder

2 Tbls. shortening or oil

2 teaspoons active dry yeast

Directions:

- Once you have made the dough let it rise.
- Cut the dough into four equal parts, then cut each fourth into four equal parts. (There should be 16 pieces - piece should be approximately 2 oz.)
- Roll into a ball and place into a greased cupcake tin or baking dish
- Bake in oven at 350°F for 18-20 minutes
- Smother with butter (optional)

Cornbread
Makes 6 muffins

1 cup flour (can be whole wheat flour)

1 cup freshly ground cornmeal (can use dent corn or pop corn)

1/4 cup brown or white sugar

1/4 cup powdered margarine or powdered butter

1 Tbls. powdered milk or powdered buttermilk

2 Tbls. powdered eggs

1/2 tsp. baking soda

1/2 tsp. baking powder

1/2 tsp. salt

1 1/2 Cups water

Directions:

Mix all powdered ingredients
together then add water

Mix until smooth

Pour into a greased muffin tin

Bake at 350°F for 20-25 minutes

Smother With Butter
And Enjoy!

Make An Instant Dry Mix:

Mix all the dried ingredients together in a mixing bowl.

Place in a Ziploc bag until ready to use.

To mix add 1 cup of water to 2 cups mix (1 part water to 2 part mix)

Bake at 350 degrees for 20-25 minutes

For a moist Corn Muffin mix 1 to 1

Corn is harder and is higher in moisture content than typical storage wheat. Dent Corn that is readily available or for that matter, any dried corn will work, you can even use popcorn to make your corn flour, there are some who prefer popcorn. I have used dried corn from my garden and milled it with excellent success. When I grind corn in my mill I will then follow it with an equal amount of wheat. This gets the corn out of the stones and I have a 50-50 mix of corn and wheat flour ready to use in my cornbread.

In order to put this recipe to use in your preparedness program you must store popcorn or dent corn that you can make into corn flour. Refer to the cornbread recipe to extend the quantities you will need.

 For example: if you prepare cornbread once a week for 50 weeks then you will need 50 cups of corn to make into flour. Which would be a little more than 3 gallons of corn. You should probably consider buying a 5 gallon bucket of dent corn and you can use it throughout the year. When it is half gone purchase another one and you will always have a year's supply of dent corn for making your cornbread. Finally transfer the cornbread ingredient totals to the grand total inventory page.

You can see how very important it is that you know how you will use your preparedness pantry in order to fill your preparedness pantry with the proper items and the correct quantities.

TIP:

Use 50% white flour and 50% whole wheat flower to ease your family into whole wheat. A 50# bag of popcorn is easily purchased and contains about 6 1/2 gallons.

Homemade Soups And Stews

In most cases lunch is typically not considered the main meal of the day. A varied yet simple collection of lunch recipes is essential for a complete preparedness plan. In this section we will consider a few examples.

Remember that each recipe must be easily prepared from your preparedness pantry with items that are readily available in the market.

The main intent of this book is to teach correct principals of a preparedness pantry and that will allow you to determine your own personal needs. By now you should have a good idea about how to take a recipe and transfer it to your preparedness pantry.

As you continue with this section, keep in mind that you should begin to add your own recipe ideas for your family. You now know how to figure the quantities for what you must store to include a recipe into your pantry so you can expand your selections as you try new recipes.

Homemade Dried Tomato Soup

Ingredients:

2/3 cup dried tomatoes (Crush and pack them in)

2/3 cup powdered milk (must be powdered milk)

3 Cup water

2 Tbls. butter or margarine

1/8 tsp. baking soda

Season: salt, pepper and spices to taste

Directions:

- Combine tomatoes, powdered milk and water into blender, bled well (This will make soup thick).

- Heat in 1 qt. saucepan (do not let boil).

- Season soup as desired.

- When hot stir in butter and 1/8 tsp. baking soda (Soda is to neutralize the tomato acid).

- This recipe can be doubled or tripled, however soda does not have to be increased.

Seasoning Suggestions:

- Salt
- Pepper
- Dried Onion
- Oregano
- Basil
- Italian seasoning mix

Canned soups are an excellent preparedness food and should be a vital part of your preparedness pantry.

Basic "Cream Of Soup"

Ingredients:

    2 cups powder milk

    3/4 cup cornstarch

    2 Tbls. Dried onion

    1/2 tsp. pepper

    1/4 cup chicken bouillon powder

    (exchange for other soups)

Directions:

- Combine milk, cornstarch, onion flakes, pepper and chicken bouillon.
- Mix well and store in the refrigerator or freezer for future use.
- For condensed soup mix 1 part mix to 2 parts water
- For regular soup mix 1 part mix to 4 parts water
- For a can of "Cream of Soup:" Use 1/2 cup mix and 1 Cup water
- To Cook: Put in saucepan and cook on medium heat, stir until thickened.

Options:

For cream of mushroom replace bouillon with dried mushrooms

For cream of celery replace bouillon with crushed dried celery

1 teaspoon dried basil (optional)

1/4 teaspoon dried thyme

Use this recipe to make "cream of soup" for dinner preparations, be sure to add the totals to your grand totals.

Potato Soup In A Jar

Makes 24 servings

Ingredients:

6 Cups Instant potatoes

5 Cups Powdered milk

1/2 Cup dried onion flakes

1/2 Cup Chicken Bouillon

1 Tbl. Dried Parsley

1/2 tsp. Thyme

Directions:

Mix well the above ingredients and keep in a re-sealable bag, store in the refrigerator for longer life.

Into 1 cup boiling water add 1/2 cup dry potato soup mix.
Season with salt and pepper as desired.

Options:

Add cooked vegetables

Mix in some powdered cheese

Stir in instant Raman Noodles

Add egg noodles

More Lunch Ideas

Raman Noodles are one item with which we are all familiar. I think it is a staple for college students. They can be a nice hot meal or you can stir them into a hot soup. They store well and are easy to prepare. One word of caution, Raman Noodles are not all created equal, some have an excellent taste and some are not that good. My recommendation is that you try them out and buy the ones you *will* eat. You can prolong the storage life by placing the un-opened packages in a one-gallon re-sealable bag.

Dried soup mixes are another excellent choice for long-term storage. Once again they are easy to acquire, they are easy to prepare, you simply add boiling water.

Peanut butter, an excellent source of protein, jams and jellies are additional items to have in your preparedness pantry. They can be used as sandwich spreads, in pancakes and muffins. Jams can also be added to your oatmeal and wheat cereals as a sweetener. Determine your needs and add the totals to the worksheet.

The typical PB&J sandwich will use 2-3 Tbls. each of peanut butter and jelly.

Lunch and Bread Menu Total Volume Table

Now it's time to bring it all together for lunch and bread.

Enter quantities needed for each menu preparation from your choices then extend to grand TOTAL for your preparedness needs.

Mark "t" teaspoons, "T" Tablespoons or "C" cups above input number

#Preparations																							
Ingredients	Bread			Rolls			Cornbread														Grad Total		
	t	T	C	t	T	C	t	T	C	t	T	C	t	T	C	t	T	C	t	T	C
	t	T	C	t	T	C	t	T	C	t	T	C	t	T	C	t	T	C	t	T	C
Baking Powder	t	T	C	t	T	C	t	T	C	t	T	C	t	T	C	t	T	C	t	T	C
Baking Soda	t	T	C	t	T	C	t	T	C	t	T	C	t	T	C	t	T	C	t	T	C
Butter, Powdered	t	T	C	t	T	C	t	T	C	t	T	C	t	T	C	t	T	C	t	T	C
Buttermilk Powder	t	T	C	t	T	C	t	T	C	t	T	C	t	T	C	t	T	C	t	T	C
Catsup	t	T	C	t	T	C	t	T	C	t	T	C	t	T	C	t	T	C	t	T	C
Corn, Dent	t	T	C	t	T	C	t	T	C	t	T	C	t	T	C	t	T	C	t	T	C
Corn, Pop	t	T	C	t	T	C	t	T	C	t	T	C	t	T	C	t	T	C	t	T	C
Eggs, Powdered	t	T	C	t	T	C	t	T	C	t	T	C	t	T	C	t	T	C	t	T	C
Flour, Baking	t	T	C	t	T	C	t	T	C	t	T	C	t	T	C	t	T	C	t	T	C
Honey	t	T	C	t	T	C	t	T	C	t	T	C	t	T	C	t	T	C	t	T	C
Jam/Jelly	t	T	C	t	T	C	t	T	C	t	T	C	t	T	C	t	T	C	t	T	C
Margarine, Powdered	t	T	C	t	T	C	t	T	C	t	T	C	t	T	C	t	T	C	t	T	C
Milk, Powdered	t	T	C	t	T	C	t	T	C	t	T	C	t	T	C	t	T	C	t	T	C

	t	T	c	t	T	C	t	T	C	t	T	C	t	T	C	t	T	C	t	T	C
Noodles																					
Peanut Butter																					
Raman Noodles																					
Salsa																					
Salt																					
Shortening/ Oil, Powdered																					
Soup Mix, Dried																					
Spaghetti																					
Sugar, Brown																					
Sugar, Granulated																					
Syrup																					
Tomatoes, Dried																					
Wheat, Flour																					
Wheat, Storage																					
Yeast, Dried																					

See Appendix F

It's Your Turn

It's your turn to create a few of your own recipes. Now you know what is important. You know how to fit product into your preparedness program and daily menus.

Write down your recipes on the next few pages. Make sure that they fit the preparedness criterion:

Preparedness pantry items should be:
- Easy to store
- Easy to acquire
- Easy to prepare

Once you have written down your recipe then determine how many times in 365 days you will serve that preparation. Be sure to adjust the quantities for the size of your family.

Finally transfer the totals to the *Lunch and Bread Menu Total Volume Table* by listing your menu by name and adding the totals to the grand total.
(See Appendix C)

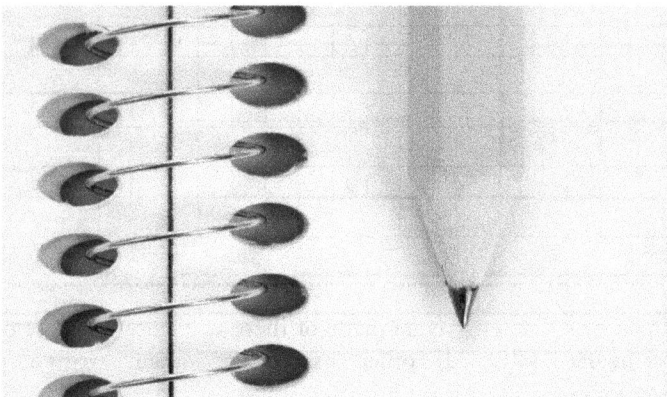

Your Recipe

Your Recipe

Your Recipe

Your Recipe

Your Recipe

Your Recipe

DINNER IDEAS

Dinner Ideas

Most people consider dinner to be their main meal of the day. I would imagine it is not as important to have your meals in perfect order as it is to have a well-balanced diet and having specifically enough to eat to be healthy. Therefore your survival preparedness menus may be different from what you eat on a daily basis nevertheless, you need to be familiar with your preparedness menu and have the ability to prepare them efficiently. You should also include having the proper cooking tools.

In this section we will be discussing various items that you may include in your preparedness dinner menu. Some of these items may also be used for breakfast and lunch. As you continue to catch the vision of creating a preparedness pantry you will come up with many more ideas and with this system you can easily add virtually any recipe to your preparedness menu list. So the premise is; that you are taught to fish or to prepare properly so you can eat in time of crisis!

Macaroni and Cheese

Macaroni and cheese is an excellent item to have in your preparedness pantry. This recipe can be prepared with all dried ingredients, just add water and a few vegetables. Finally add a can of tuna fish and you have an easy to prepare stove top meal all from your preparedness pantry that your whole family will love. You can even add this recipe to your daily dinner menu and it will quickly become a family favorite.

Ingredients:

1 Cup Elbow Macaroni

2 Tbsp. Powdered Cheese

1 Tbsp. Powdered Butter

1 Tbsp. Powdered milk

Cook noodles, pour off all but about 1/8 C. water

Stir in powdered cheese, milk and butter

Variations:

Add 1 can tuna fish

Add breadcrumbs or potato chips

Add I biscuit Shredded Wheat

Add cooked peas or corn

Make a cheese mix for small servings of Macaroni and Cheese Dinners plus you can use this mix as a cheese sauce in your cooking:

      1/2 Cup Powdered Cheese

      1/4 Cup Powdered Milk

      1/4 Cup Powdered Butter

Fill up a large re-sealable bag with the above ratios of ingredients, mix well and use it as a cheese sauce by adding water or by stirring it into many dishes.

For smaller portions of Macaroni and Cheese Dinners cook 1/4 Cup Elbow Macaroni then mix 1 Tbsp. of the above mix over mostly drained and cooked macaroni. For each 1/4 cup of uncooked Elbow Macaroni sprinkle 1 Tbsp. of this mix over the cooked macaroni.

You can also store the pre-packaged Macaroni and Cheese dinners. Be sure you also use the same process in figuring your needs by determining how many times in one year you will be serving Macaroni and Cheese as part of a meal and how many people one package will serve.

The Mac & Cheese recipe is ideal for 3 or 4 people so to add this to your preparedness pantry program you need to determine how many times you will make this preparation for your family over the next 365 days. Let's assume that you will do 50 preparations. If that is the case you will need to store 50 cups of noodles or slightly over 3 gallons. You will also add to your preparedness pantry an additional 100 Tablespoons of powdered cheese, 50 Tablespoons of powdered milk and 50 Tablespoons of powdered butter. That would mean 6 1/2 cups of powdered cheese and 3 1/4 cups of both powdered milk and powdered butter for this preparation.

Mac N' Cheese Thermos Dinner
Makes 2 servings

Yes! You read it right, Mac N' Cheese in the thermos! All you need is boiling water.

Ingredients:

1/2 Cup Elbow Macaroni
1 1/2 Cups Boiling Water

Directions:

*   Put macaroni into thermos then add boiling water. Seal the thermos
*   Shake the thermos to *stir* the macaroni inside
*   Open thermos after 30 minutes.
*   Pour off water into a cup
*   Pour cooked macaroni into serving bowl
*   Add back 2-4 Tbls. of drained water as needed for creaminess
*   Stir in 2 Tbls. of cheese mix from previous page
*   Season with a pinch of salt if desired

Do not let Macaroni sit in water past cooking time as it will become soggy. Sure you can cook macaroni on the stove quickly, but this is an alternative to be aware of if resources are limited. If by chance you are under a "boil water order" you are ready to cook after the required time of boiling.

This example is given to illustrate that a thermos can be an alternative cooking option.

Tuna And Rice Dinner

Serves six

Ingredients:

1 Can Tuna

1 1/2 Cup Frozen Peas or (1 can of peas) or (3/4 cup of dried peas plus 1 Cup of water)

1/2 Cup milk or (1 Tbsp. powdered milk plus just under 1/2 Cup of water)

1 Can Cream of Mushroom Soup

1 Cup Brown Rice (any rice but do not use instant)

Directions:

- Add rice to a rice cooker or saucepan with 2 cups of water
- Place Tuna, Cream of Mushroom Soup, Peas and Milk into a different saucepan and cook over medium heat until hot. Do not let boil
- Remove from heat and cover with lid until rice is done.
- Stir in the rice when done or just pour it over a plate of rice.

Cook this recipe for your family to try and if this is one of the recipes you choose then add to your master list the ingredients that you will need.

If you were to prepare 75 preparations of this recipe for example: you would then need 75 cans of tuna fish, 75 cans of peas or the appropriate quantity of dry peas, you'll need 75 Tablespoons of powdered milk, which is 4 1/4 cups. And finally you will need 75 cans of cream of mushroom soup and 75 cups of rice added to your preparedness pantry.

See Appendix H for example worksheet

Variations:

Use Green beans or corn in place of peas (tally any variations you wish to make and add them to your preparedness pantry).

Pour over or mix into cooked macaroni or noodles rather than rice.

Top toasted bread for another variation.

Tuna And Noodle Casserole

This recipe will come to be a family favorite, everybody likes tuna fish and everybody likes noodles. As you can see all of the ingredients that you need are easily stored in your preparedness pantry. Add the totals of this recipe to the grand total of your preparedness needs, serve it regularly and if hard times demand that you live off your preparedness pantry exclusively you are ready and know what to do.

Ingredients:

1 Can Cream of Mushroom Soup

1/2 cup milk or (1 Tbl. powdered milk just under 1/2 Cup water)

1 cup Peas of (1/2 cup of dried peas plus 1/2 cup water)

1 or 2 cans tuna, drained

2 cups medium egg noodles, cooked and drained

1 Tbl. Melted butter (Or 1 Tbl. Butter powder plus 1 Tbl. of water)

2 Tbls. Dry bread crumbs or potato chips (to top when done)

Directions:

- Preheat oven to 350°F
- Stir the soup, milk, peas, tuna, melted butter and the cooked and drained noodles into a 1 1/2-quart casserole dish.
- Bake the tuna and noodle preparation for 20 minutes or until hot and bubbling. Stir then sprinkle the breadcrumbs on top of casserole.
- Bake for 5 minutes or until the breadcrumbs are golden brown.

Recipe Options:

For Chicken Noodle Casserole, substitute **2 cups** cubed cooked chopped chicken for the tuna.

Sprinkle in dried tomato flakes or some dried chili for added seasoning.

Top with grated cheese.

Replace peas with corn or green beans.

This recipe can be made from reconstituted peas (1/2 cup dried make 1 cup). You can also make homemade noodles and homemade cream of mushroom soup. Make your own breadcrumbs by toasting bread or drying bread in the sun or leave it out and serve the bread on the side.

Stove Top Method:

Cook Noodles and peas on stove

Drain water

Add soup, milk, tuna and butter and stir

Sprinkle breadcrumbs over top

Place lit on pan to retain heat

Vegetables And Rice

Vegetables and Casseroles are very easy to prepare this makes them a very good preparedness option because you are using energy to cook only one item rather than cooking four separate dishes one at a time.

Ingredients:

1 can Cream of Chicken Soup (any "cream of" soup will do)

4 cups water

1 cup rice, (Brown, Jasmine, Parboiled)

1 teaspoon lemon pepper ... Other seasoning as desired

1/4 Cup each of the following dried vegetables: (use 1/2 cup for fresh or canned)

- Celery
- Carrots
- Broccoli
- Green beans
- Peas
- Tomato powder

1/2 Cup of dried Corn

4-6 skinless, boneless chicken breast halves, cut into bite-size pieces or leave whole (2 -4 cups of other meat for variety)

Optional Topper - 1/2 cup shredded Cheddar cheese (spread on top after done)

78

Directions:

- Pre-heat the oven to 230°F. Stir the soup, water, rice, onion powder, lemon pepper seasoning, and vegetables in a 2-quart shallow baking dish.
- Top with the chicken. Season the chicken as desired. Cover the baking dish with foil or lid.
- Bake in oven for 3 hours at 230°F. The chicken should be cooked through and the rice and vegetables tender. (Especially check the dried carrots)
- Top with shredded cheese as desired. Cover again with foil and let the casserole stand for 10 minutes.

Variations:

Use other meats such as Turkey, Pork, Rabbit, or even ground beef. Vary the types of cheeses. Try different rice's or mix several varieties. Add Jalapeños, chili seeds or other spicy seasonings.

Vegetable Stew
Serves 12

Here is an excellent vegetable stew recipe, you do not have to put in all the variety that is shown in the recipe you can put in whatever you like this recipe calls for about 3 cups of dried vegetables. If you are drying your own vegetables mix them however you would like and follow the rest of the recipe. You can also use canned or fresh vegetables with and adjustment to the volume.

Ingredients:

1/4 Cup of the following dried vegetables:

- Celery
- Broccoli
- Peas
- Carrots
- Green Beans
- Tomato Powder

1/2 Cup of dried Corn

1 Can Cream of Chicken Soup or (cream of celery or mushroom)

5-6 Cups water

1 t. chicken of beef bouillon (optional)

1T Lemon Pepper (Season as you like)

2 Cups chopped cooked chicken or turkey

Directions:

In Crock-pot cook on high for 2 1/2 hours or until vegetable are soft.

Add 2 Cups chopped cooked chicken or turkey, cook in crock-pot 30 more minutes.

For Variety:

Add ¼ C. Barley or Brown Rice or 1 T. Soy beans at time of soaking (Add ½ C. extra water)

Add ¼ C. noodles or instant rice to crock pot last 30 min of cooking time (Add ½ C. extra water)

Stove Method:

Soak for 4-6 hours then simmer on stove until vegetables are cooked (about 1 hour)

Certainly you can think of ways you can modify it this basic recipe. Add ground beef, bar-b-q sauce. Try adding some pork ribs or just have a vegetable stew full of zingy spices on a cold winter day!

Be creative and you will find many uses for your mix!

Spaghetti / Pasta

1 Cup Flour (can be half wheat and half white or all whole wheat)

1 Large egg

2 T Water or milk or olive oil (Substitute milk and egg as follows: 2 T Powder egg, 1 1/2 t powdered milk + 1/4 Cup water)

½ t salt (optional)

OR For A Larger Batch

4 Cups flour

4 eggs

2 T Water or milk or olive oil

1 t salt (optional)

Directions:

- Stir all ingredients into a bowl until it makes a ball.
- Knead the dough until even and firm.
- You may add a drop or water or oil if needed but dough must be stiff, it is easy to add too much liquid.
- Wrap in plastic and let dough rest for 20 minutes (extremely important to allow gluten to start working).
- Roll out dough, cut or run through pasta machine as desired.
- Let dry or cook right away!
- Cook as any spaghetti product however, since it is not dried but fresh it will cook much faster, test to see when it is cooked.

Beans

Beans have some good qualities and also some undesirable qualities, nevertheless they should be in your long-term preparedness pantry. Beans are high in fiber, low in fat and they are a good source of protein and carbohydrates. Because of their relative low cost, beans provide good nutrition for very little money, and they will store well. I would suggest that you consider storing Red Kidney Beans, Pinto Beans, Black Beans, and White Beans. These can be easily purchased and then stored for long periods of time. Whole or mashed beans can be added to meatloaves, soups, stews or casseroles.

Because of the lack of one or more amino acids in plant proteins that are contained in animal protein, beans should be paired with either an animal protein or another plant protein. For example: Beans may be paired with seeds and nuts or with a grain (wheat, cornmeal, rice, oats, etc.)

TIP:

Beans must be cooked completely before eating. Sprouting your beans before eating will increase the nutrients many times over.

Gas From Beans

Gas is frankly an undesirable side effect of eating beans. The body lacks enzymes to digest some sugars in the beans. Undigested sugars ferment in the stomach and create gas. Now you know!

Here are a few ways to help alleviate undesirable gas:

1. Soak beans minimum 3 hours preferably 8-12 hours; discard the water.

2 Sprout beans by soaking beans 12 hours then change water twice a day for 3-4 days until the beans begin to sprout.

3. Use a product like "Beano" to add the lacking enzymes.

4. It is widely believed that eating beans on a regular basis will help your body develop that needed enzymes.

Directions:

First soak the beans as follows: Cover with two to three times as much water as beans then soak 12 to 20 hours in cool place. When soaking is complete discard soaking water.

Cooking Beans

Remember that beans will double or triple in volume during soaking and cooking. Therefore one cup of beans will produce as much as 3 cups cooked. The slower beans are cooked the easier they will be to digest. The easiest way to cook beans is in a crockpot. If it is necessary to add water to the cooking beans first bring the water to be added to a boil before then add the boiling water. Adding cold water to boiling beans will toughen the beans and slow down the cooking process.

TIP:

The older the beans the tougher they are and the less digestible. Here are some ideas to soften older beans:

- *Cook and freeze. The freezing moisture in the bean will create softer beans.*
- *Pressure cook as per the manufacture's directions. Increase cooking time as needed to produce the desired texture.*
- *Soak and cook older beans for twice as long*

Follow this formula for figuring your suggested bean needs:

1/4 cup dried beans will yield a serving of 1/2 to 3/4 cup of cooked beans.

Take the number in your family times the number of preparations (meals or days) you will serve beans. Divide that number by 4 to get the total number of cups of beans to keep in storage.

5 (number in family) **X 150** (meals or days) = **750** ÷ 4 (1/4 cup dried beans/serving) = **187 1/2** cups of beans.

To convert to gallons ÷ **16** (cups/gallon) =**11.7 gallons**. This would mean that you must maintain in your preparedness pantry at least 12 gallons of various beans.

In the worksheet we have four bean choices listed, Pinto, Black, White Red Kidney beans. You may add others that you prefer and divide your needs up among the choices.

Example:

Pinto – 5 Gallons

Black – 2 Gallons

White – 2 Gallons

Red Kidney – 3 Gallons

The total is 12 gallons to meet the storage needs. It would be a good idea to have a little extra. It's the same idea that that you have more gas in your car than you need for the trip. The calculations are the minimum you need to maintain your needs. Your first goal should be to obtain the minimum quantities needed then a surplus of 10% to 25% or even more can be added.

Now figure you family's needs and add them to the Grand Total Worksheet! (See Appendix C)

One gallon of beans weighs about 8 pounds. A 5-gallon bucket weighs 40 pounds. In the above example you would need to purchase a rounded off 100 pounds of beans.

Rice

Rice is the most commonly eaten food in the world. There are over 7000 varieties of rice produced throughout the world and what you choose to store will largely be determined by where you live and availability. For many people rice is the main staple in their diet and also can be a means of barter or exchange. Rice is a whole grain and is a good source of energy, vitamins and minerals.

Brown rice – Brown rice is a whole grain, it is an unpolished grain of rice in which only the outer fibrous inedible hull is removed. Brown rice requires a little more water and longer cooking time than white rice. It has a chewy texture, and a nutty flavor. Brown rice's shelf life is shorter because of the high fat content. It is not the best choice for long-term storage.

Milled White rice – With white rice the hulls or germ, the outer bran layers and most of the inner bran are removed in the milling process. During this process a loss of 10% of protein, 85% of the fat and 70% of the minerals and because of this it is enriched to partially replace the lost nutrients. This rice stores well and is typically the cheapest. The Jasmine variety is readily available and can be purchased at the club stores in large bags at about 2/3 the typical price at the grocery store.

Parboiled rice – This rice is also called processed or converted rice. It has been cooked before milling by a special steam pressure process. This process also pushes the nutrients into the grain. A longer cooking time is needed than white rice, but after cooking the grains will be fluffier. Parboiled is also readily available and can also be purchased in large bags at a 2/3 saving at the club stores.

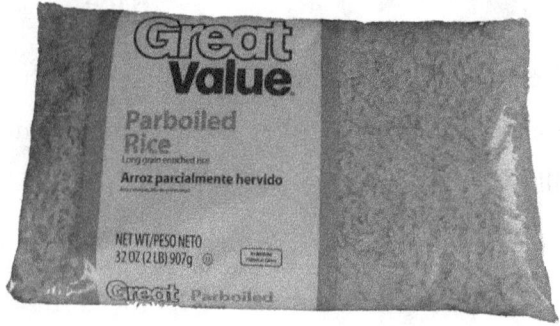

Instant or Minute – This rice is completely cooked then dried for future cooking. It needs only to be stirred into boiling water to be ready for serving. This rice is never cooked. Any store will have a variety of choices of instant rice. The biggest advantage of this rice is that it prepares quickly and with little cooking energy.

Directions:

Here are some important rules in preparing rice. Improper handling will result in the loss of nutrients and the a poorer eating quality of rice:

1. **Do not** wash or rinse rice before cooking or rinse it after cooking. Rice is already clean. Nutrients on the surface of the rice will be washed away if it is washed or rinsed before cooking.

2. **Do not** use too much water when cooking rice. Any water drained off means wasted food value. Too much water makes the rice soggy. Too little water results in dry rice. (The *general* rule on rice is: "1 part rice 2 parts water equal 3 parts cooked rice")

3. **Do not** stir rice after the rice comes to a boil. This will break up the grains and your rice then may become extra sticky and less desirable.

4. **Do not** leave rice in the pan in which it is cooked for more than 5-10 minutes or the cooked rice will pack.

Follow this formula for figuring your suggested Rice needs:

1/4 cup dried rice will yield a serving of approximately 3/4 cup of cooked rice.

Take the number in your family times the number of times (meals or days) you will serve rice in your preparedness program. Then divide that number by 3 to get the total number of uncooked cups of rice to keep in your preparedness pantry.

5 (number in family) **X** 150 (meals or days) = **750** ÷ **3** (1/4 cup dried rice/serving) = **250 cups of rice**

To convert to gallons ÷ 16 (cups/gallon) = **15.625 gallons** (15 5/8 gallons). This would mean that you must maintain in your preparedness storage at least 16 gallons of various rice's.

In the worksheet we have four rice choices listed, Jasmine (a white variety), Brown (whole grain), Parboiled (converted rice), and Instant or minute rice. You may add others that you prefer and divide your needs up among the choices.

Example:

Jasmine (white) – 6 Gallons

Brown – 3 Gallons

Parboiled – 4 Gallons

Instant or Minute – 3 Gallons

The total is 16 gallons to meet the storage needs. It would be a good idea to have a little extra. It's the same idea that you have more gas in your can than you need for the trip. These calculations are the minimum you need to maintain for your needs. Your first goal should be the minimum quantities needed then a surplus of 10% to 25% or even more can be added.

One gallon of rice weighs just less than 8 pounds. A 5-gallon bucket then weighs approximately 40 pounds. In the above example you would need to purchase a rounded off 130 pounds of rice.

Now figure you family's needs and add them to the Grand Total Worksheet! Slowly you are moving forward towards a complete preparedness pantry.

Potatoes

Instant potatoes are easy to find, easy to prepare and easy to store, this makes potato flakes an excellent choice for the preparedness pantry. There are three types of potatoes to discuss, potato flakes, potato pearls and potato granules, the last two are used more commercially however they are excellent, easily prepared and available in many club stores. My personal best choice is the granular they are easily made by just adding water. They are excellent for camping, they can be added to soups as a thickener and additionally used to supplement flour in baking.

Potato Flakes

Grocery stores have many choices of potato flakes. Determine your favorite then build your potato storage from there. Potato flakes are made with milk and butter added. If you choose to have potato flakes in your preparedness pantry you will also need to add additional butter, milk and salt.

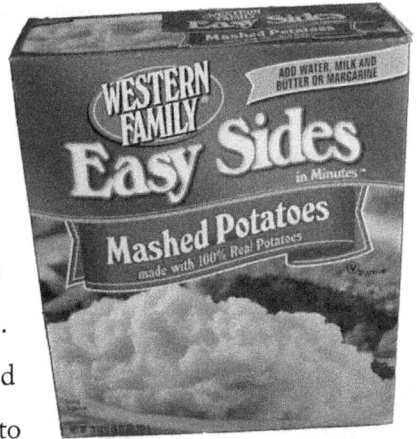

Typical Directions For Potato Flakes:
This recipe makes six servings.

1. In a sauce pan mix 2 cups of water, 3/4 teaspoon of salt plus 3 Tbls. of butter or margarine
2. Bring water to boil
3. Remove from heat and add 2/3 cup of milk and 2 cups of flakes.
4. Stir with a fork to moisten.

Potato Pearls

Potato pearls are served as mashed potatoes in many food service settings. They are easy to prepare and only require water. The taste is excellent and they provide you with a rich source of carbohydrates. Potato pearls are an excellent preparedness pantry choice because they only need water to prepare, they are easy to find and they are easy to store.

Typical Directions for potato pearls:

- Into 1/2 cup of boiling water stir in 1/4 cup of potato pearls.
- Let the potatoes sit 3-5 minutes and they are ready to serve.

You can see why they are a restaurant's favorite, and also is a great choice for the preparedness pantry. Because potato pearls contain butter, which is oil, the shelf life will be shorter. Refer to the manufacture for suggested life.

One 28 oz. bag of potato pearls will make about 40 servings so with a little math you can determine your storage needs.

There are two ways to figure the needs. One is to determine how many servings you want then divide that number by 40 and that will determine how many 28 oz. bags you need to store. The other way would be to take the total number of servings and multiply by .75 and the answer will be the number of ounces you will need to store.

Here is an example of the first method:

You have determined that your family of five will serve 190 meals including potatoes. Then **190** (number of meals) **X 5** (number in family) = **950** (total servings) ÷ **40** (servings per 28 oz. bag) = **23 3/4 28 oz. bags.** Now you know that 24 bags of potato pearls should be maintained in your preparedness pantry for your family of five.

Potato Granules

This is another preparedness item that has many uses. Potato granules come as a fine powder that is mixed with boiling water to yield a food similar in texture and taste to mashed potatoes. Potatoes are an excellent source of carbohydrates (energy) and given the ease of preparation and minimal cooking fuel to prepare. Potato granules should be a main item in the preparedness pantry. Potato granules can be mixed with milk powder to provide additional protein and increase palatability.

Among other uses, potato granules can be used to thicken soups and stews. Use them for camping: heat water, stir in granules then a little butter and there is a high energy easy to pack easy to prepare food!

A five-gallon bucket of potato granules weighs 40 pounds and provides 600 servings. That would afford a family of five 120 meals worth of potatoes. Sample the different types of potatoes that are available to determine which you like best then fill up the preparedness pantry! These may be difficult to find but they are great to have.

Dinner Menu Total Volume Table

Now it's time to bring it all together for dinner.

Enter quantities needed for each menu preparation from your choices then extend to grand TOTAL for your preparedness needs. See Appendix F

Mark "t" teaspoons, "T" Tablespoons or "C" cups above input number

#Preparations Ingredients																					Grad Total		
Baking Powder	t	T	c	t	T	c	t	T	c	t	T	c	t	T	c	t	T	c	t	T	c
Baking Soda	t	T	c	t	T	c	t	T	c	t	T	c	t	T	c	t	T	c	t	T	c
Beans, Black	t	T	c	t	T	c	t	T	c	t	T	c	t	T	c	t	T	c	t	T	c
Beans, Pinto	t	T	c	t	T	c	t	T	c	t	T	c	t	T	c	t	T	c	t	T	c
Beans, Red Kidney	t	T	c	t	T	c	t	T	c	t	T	c	t	T	c	t	T	c	t	T	c
Beans, White	t	T	c	t	T	c	t	T	c	t	T	c	t	T	c	t	T	c	t	T	c
Bullion, Beef	t	T	c	t	T	c	t	T	c	t	T	c	t	T	c	t	T	c	t	T	c
Butter, Powdered	t	T	c	t	T	c	t	T	c	t	T	c	t	T	c	t	T	c	t	T	c
Buttermilk Powder	t	T	c	t	T	c	t	T	c	t	T	c	t	T	c	t	T	c	t	T	c
Catsup	t	T	c	t	T	c	t	T	c	t	T	c	t	T	c	t	T	c	t	T	c
Cheese, Powdered	t	T	c	t	T	c	t	T	c	t	T	c	t	T	c	t	T	c	t	T	c
Corn Starch	t	T	c	t	T	c	t	T	c	t	T	c	t	T	c	t	T	c	t	T	c
Eggs, Powdered	t	T	c	t	T	c	t	T	c	t	T	c	t	T	c	t	T	c	t	T	c
Flour, Baking	t	T	c	t	T	c	t	T	c	t	T	c	t	T	c	t	T	c	t	T	c
Honey	t	T	c	t	T	c	t	T	c	t	T	c	t	T	c	t	T	c	t	T	c

Item																								
Jam/Jelly	t	T	c	t	T	c	t	T	c	t	T	c	t	T	c	t	T	c	t	T	c	t	T	c
Macaroni	t	T	c	t	T	c	t	T	c	t	T	c	t	T	c	t	T	c	t	T	c	t	T	c
Milk, Powdered	t	T	c	t	T	c	t	T	c	t	T	c	t	T	c	t	T	c	t	T	c	t	T	c
Noodles	t	T	c	t	T	c	t	T	c	t	T	c	t	T	c	t	T	c	t	T	c	t	T	c
Peas, Dried	t	T	c	t	T	c	t	T	c	t	T	c	t	T	c	t	T	c	t	T	c	t	T	c
Potatoes, Flakes	t	T	c	t	T	c	t	T	c	t	T	c	t	T	c	t	T	c	t	T	c	t	T	c
Potatoes, Granules	t	T	c	t	T	c	t	T	c	t	T	c	t	T	c	t	T	c	t	T	c	t	T	c
Potatoes, Pearls	t	T	c	t	T	c	t	T	c	t	T	c	t	T	c	t	T	c	t	T	c	t	T	c
Rice, Brown	t	T	c	t	T	c	t	T	c	t	T	c	t	T	c	t	T	c	t	T	c	t	T	c
Rice, Jasmine	t	T	c	t	T	c	t	T	c	t	T	c	t	T	c	t	T	c	t	T	c	t	T	c
Rice, Parboiled	t	T	c	t	T	c	t	T	c	t	T	c	t	T	c	t	T	c	t	T	c	t	T	c
Salsa	t	T	c	t	T	c	t	T	c	t	T	c	t	T	c	t	T	c	t	T	c	t	T	c
Salt	t	T	c	t	T	c	t	T	c	t	T	c	t	T	c	t	T	c	t	T	c	t	T	c
Shortening/ Oil, Powdered	t	T	c	t	T	c	t	T	c	t	T	c	t	T	c	t	T	c	t	T	c	t	T	c
Soup, Cream Of Celery	t	T	c	t	T	c	t	T	c	t	T	c	t	T	c	t	T	c	t	T	c	t	T	c
Soup, Cream of Chicken	t	T	c	t	T	c	t	T	c	t	T	c	t	T	c	t	T	c	t	T	c	t	T	c
Soup, Cream of Mushroom	t	T	c	t	T	c	t	T	c	t	T	c	t	T	c	t	T	c	t	T	c	t	T	c
Soup, Tomato	t	T	c	t	T	c	t	T	c	t	T	c	t	T	c	t	T	c	t	T	c	t	T	c
Sugar, Brown	t	T	c	t	T	c	t	T	c	t	T	c	t	T	c	t	T	c	t	T	c	t	T	c
Sugar, Granulated	t	T	c	t	T	c	t	T	c	t	T	c	t	T	c	t	T	c	t	T	c	t	T	c

Syrup, Corn	t	T	c	t	T	c	t	T	c	t	T	c	t	T	c	t	T	c	t	T	c
Tomatoes, Dried	t	T	c	t	T	c	t	T	c	t	T	c	t	T	c	t	T	c	t	T	c
Tuna Fish	t	T	c	t	T	c	t	T	c	t	T	c	t	T	c	t	T	c	t	T	c
Wheat, Flour	t	T	c	t	T	c	t	T	c	t	T	c	t	T	c	t	T	c	t	T	c
Wheat, Storage	t	T	c	t	T	c	t	T	c	t	T	c	t	T	c	t	T	c	t	T	c
Yeast, Dried	t	T	c	t	T	c	t	T	c	t	T	c	t	T	c	t	T	c	t	T	c
	t	T	c	t	T	c	t	T	c	t	T	c	t	T	c	t	T	c	t	T	c
	t	T	c	t	T	c	t	T	c	t	T	c	t	T	c	t	T	c	t	T	c
	t	T	c	t	T	c	t	T	c	t	T	c	t	T	c	t	T	c	t	T	c
	t	T	c	t	T	c	t	T	c	t	T	c	t	T	c	t	T	c	t	T	c
	t	T	c	t	T	c	t	T	c	t	T	c	t	T	c	t	T	c	t	T	c
	t	T	c	t	T	c	t	T	c	t	T	c	t	T	c	t	T	c	t	T	c
	t	T	c	t	T	c	t	T	c	t	T	c	t	T	c	t	T	c	t	T	c
	t	T	c	t	T	c	t	T	c	t	T	c	t	T	c	t	T	c	t	T	c
	t	T	c	t	T	c	t	T	c	t	T	c	t	T	c	t	T	c	t	T	c
	t	T	c	t	T	c	t	T	c	t	T	c	t	T	c	t	T	c	t	T	c
	t	T	c	t	T	c	t	T	c	t	T	c	t	T	c	t	T	c	t	T	c
	t	T	c	t	T	c	t	T	c	t	T	c	t	T	c	t	T	c	t	T	c
	t	T	c	t	T	c	t	T	c	t	T	c	t	T	c	t	T	c	t	T	c
	t	T	c	t	T	c	t	T	c	t	T	c	t	T	c	t	T	c	t	T	c

Seasonings

	t	T	c	t	T	c	t	T	c	t	T	c	t	T	c	t	T	c	t	T	c
Basil																					
Cinnamon																					
Italian Seasoning Mix																					
Lemon Pepper																					
Onion																					
Oregano																					
Pepper																					

Vegetables Dried

	t	T	c	t	T	c	t	T	c	t	T	c	t	T	c	t	T	c	t	T	c
Beans																					
Broccoli																					
Carrots																					
Celery																					
Corn																					
Peas																					

Vegetables Dried (cont.)

	t	T	c	t	T	c	t	T	c	t	T	c	t	T	c	t	T	c	t	T	c
Tomatoes	t	T	c	t	T	c	t	T	c	t	T	c	t	T	c	t	T	c	t	T	c
	t	T	c	t	T	c	t	T	c	t	T	c	t	T	c	t	T	c	t	T	c
	t	T	c	t	T	c	t	T	c	t	T	c	t	T	c	t	T	c	t	T	c
	t	T	c	t	T	c	t	T	c	t	T	c	t	T	c	t	T	c	t	T	c
	t	T	c	t	T	c	t	T	c	t	T	c	t	T	c	t	T	c	t	T	c
	t	T	c	t	T	c	t	T	c	t	T	c	t	T	c	t	T	c	t	T	c
	t	T	c	t	T	c	t	T	c	t	T	c	t	T	c	t	T	c	t	T	c
	t	T	c	t	T	c	t	T	c	t	T	c	t	T	c	t	T	c	t	T	c

Sprouting Seeds

	t	T	c	t	T	c	t	T	c	t	T	c	t	T	c	t	T	c	t	T	c
Alfalfa	t	T	c	t	T	c	t	T	c	t	T	c	t	T	c	t	T	c	t	T	c
Broccoli	t	T	c	t	T	c	t	T	c	t	T	c	t	T	c	t	T	c	t	T	c
Clover	t	T	c	t	T	c	t	T	c	t	T	c	t	T	c	t	T	c	t	T	c
Peas	t	T	c	t	T	c	t	T	c	t	T	c	t	T	c	t	T	c	t	T	c
Radish	t	T	c	t	T	c	t	T	c	t	T	c	t	T	c	t	T	c	t	T	c
Wheat	t	T	c	t	T	c	t	T	c	t	T	c	t	T	c	t	T	c	t	T	c
	t	T	c	t	T	c	t	T	c	t	T	c	t	T	c	t	T	c	t	T	c
	t	T	c	t	T	c	t	T	c	t	T	c	t	T	c	t	T	c	t	T	c
	t	T	c	t	T	c	t	T	c	t	T	c	t	T	c	t	T	c	t	T	c
	t	T	c	t	T	c	t	T	c	t	T	c	t	T	c	t	T	c	t	T	c

It's Your Turn

It's your turn to create a few of your own recipes. Now you know what is important. You know how to fit product into your preparedness program and daily menus.

Write down your recipes on the next few pages. Make sure that they fit the preparedness criterion:

Preparedness pantry items should be

- Easy to store
- Easy to acquire
- Easy to prepare

Once you have written down your recipe then determine how many times in 365 days you will serve that preparation. Be sure to adjust the quantities for the size of your family.

Finally transfer the totals to the *Dinner Menu Total Volume Table* by listing your menu by name and adding the totals to the grand total.
(See Apendix A)

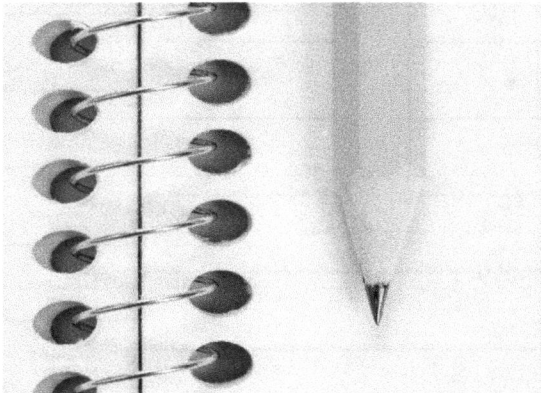

Your Recipe

Your Recipe

Your Recipe

Your Recipe

Your Recipe

Your Recipe

How To Cook Your Food In An Emergency

A very important consideration for emergency preparedness equipment is how you will cook the food. It is my suggestion that you have at least two alternative methods of cooking. You should be familiar enough with each alternative method that you can cook with ease. The alternative cooking method may also determine the recipes that you will use and therefore what you will store.

There are several methods from which to choose. Probably the most familiar is the **microwave.** Yes! The microwave that you use everyday can be an alternative method of cooking. For example if the power is out the microwave can be operated with even a small gas generator. Since microwaves are 120 volts and range between 1000 and 1500 watts. A 2000 watt generator can be purchased relatively inexpensively and will run for 8 to 10 hours on a single gallon of gasoline. This generator can also operate an electric griddle that uses up to 1500 watts. You may need to consider a generator that can operate at least a microwave and a griddle to assure this alternative method of cooking. A 25" heavy duty extension cord should also be available so the generator can be sun safely out of doors.

Bar-B-Q Grill Most everyone has bar-b-q grill and this should not be overlooked. If you intend to consider using your grill as one of your alternative cooking methods then you should have a back-up bottle of fuel full at all times. This method will do you no good if you have used up your fuel and have no replacement on hand. Make

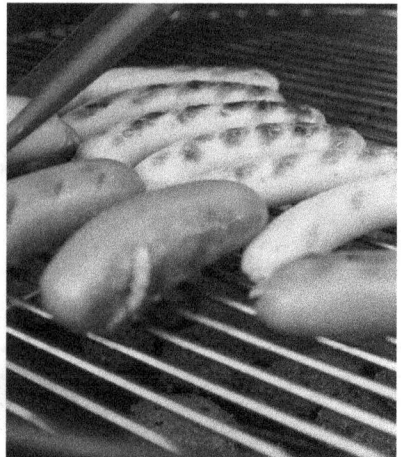

it a habit to always fill the empty bottle as soon as possible to insure that this method will be available in emergency.

Charcoal

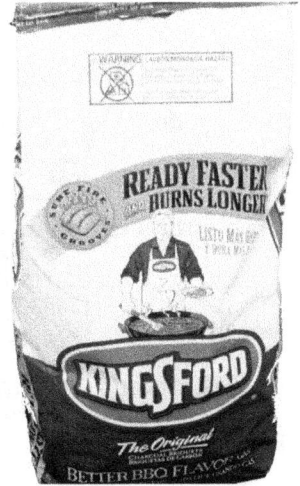

Charcoal may be the "old fashioned" method of grilling however it is still an excellent alternate source for cooking. Watch for sales on charcoal in the spring and stock-up. If you run out of propane for your grill you can make a quick emergency charcoal grill by putting charcoal in a cast iron frying pan just under the grill resting on the burners.

Camp Stoves

One of the most versatile options is the camp stove. A good sporting goods store will have many options to choose from. There are several choices of fuel; you can choose, white gas, sterno, and propane to name the most popular. One, two or even three burner stove are also available. The two burner model is probably the best option.

Be sure you also have available pots and pans that work well with your stove plus a griddle is an accessory that you will definitely be glad you have. Practice cooking a few meals on your deck or porch, the more familiar you are with your equipment the less challenging it will be when you are under pressure.

Dutch Oven

The Dutch oven is fun and perhaps carries the mystique of antique and Wild West cooking. Nevertheless once one learns the basic of Dutch oven cooking it becomes rather simple. You will need a Dutch oven or two. They will need to be seasoned as recommended by the manufacture. This alternative method is extremely efficient for cooking stews and casserole dishes. You can set-up your oven and when you return your meal is ready. If this is to be one of your alternate cooking methods then you must have an adequate supply of charcoal.

Baking Temperature Chart for Dutch Oven Cooking

Oven Top/Bottom	325°	350°	375°	400°	425°	450°
8"	15 10/5	16 11/5	17 11/6	18 12/6	19 13/6	20 14/6
10"	19 13/6	21 14/7	23 16/7	25 17/8	27 18/9	29 19/10
12"	23 16/7	25 17/8	27 18/9	29 19/10	31 21/10	33 22/11
14"	30 20/10	32 21/11	34 22/12	36 24/12	38 25/13	40 26/14

To simmer reverse briquettes to 2/3 on bottom 1/3 on top. Each briquette will produce about 10° - 15° F. worth of heat. Once you understand this chart Dutch Oven cooking becomes easy.

Dutch Oven Cooking Guidelines

- One charcoal briquette, or equally sized hot coal, will equate to approximately 10-15 degrees of heat on a fair day.
- Generally, to get a 350°F oven temperature the number of coals would be 2 times the Dutch oven diameter. A 12" oven = 24 briquettes.
- For baking, put twice as many coals on top as under the bottom. For example if the temperature calls for 15 briquettes, then put 10 on top and 5 underneath. To simmer reverse to 2/3 on bottom 1/3 on top.
- For even heat, rotate the oven and lid 90 degrees approximately halfway through recipe cooking time.
- There are about 150 briquettes in a 10 pound bag that should cook six preparations.

Hot coal quantities are approximate to maintain desired temperature you will need to replenish briquettes as they burn down.

Open Fire

An open fire is perhaps reliable but a last resort. It takes some skill to keep your heat even and is a challenge to cook your food evenly. I don't recommend this as one of your alternative cooking sources however it is a good idea to have some skill with this old method if no other resources are available.

A nice hot bed of coals can be made for your best cooking success. You may need some compatible cooking utensils and aluminum foil to aid in this method. Be sure you have "strike anywhere" matches and some fire starter.

Solar Cooking

Solar cooking can require a great deal of attention to be sure that the cooker is receiving the optimal amount of sun for best performance of the cooker. You may find yourself adjusting the oven as often as every 15 minutes.

However, not all solar ovens are created equal! For premier design and performance The SOS Sport Oven pictured here can be a life saver in an emergency. The SOS oven produces superior performance with little to no tending. Just a little practice and you can become skilled in this art. You will be cooking breads to roasts. You may even decide to cook regularly with this renewable and free energy source! Invest in an oven like this for peace of mind.

Photo Courtesy:
www.solarovens.org

Not the best, but tin foil and a cardboard box can be used to focus the sun's energy and make a homemade solar cooker that will work adequately, *if* you are willing to tend the oven. A dark colored pot with a good fitting lid is best to convert the sun's rays to heat and to retain the heat for cooking. Anything see-through or light in color will not absorb and pass though the most heat. Solar cooking will take more time to actually cook the food. Solar is a renewable energy source that needs no fuel storage, only daytime sunshine!

The Multi Fuel Stove

Possibly the most unique stove for supplemental or emergency preparedness cooking is the Volcano. This stove can cook with propane, charcoal briquettes or even firewood. This gives ultimate flexibility in your emergency cooking fuel needs, particularly in a situation where resources may become scarce. If you choose the Volcano as one of your alternate cooking sources you will want to practice with all three sources of fuel to avoid the learning curve in a stressful emergency. Fuel source versatility is one of the paramount features of this remarkable alternate cooking source.

Butane Stove

This butane stove as perhaps the best universal option for emergency cooking as far as cost is concerned. For less than $30 you can have an emergency stove and fuel that will give you several weeks of emergency cooking. The stove is easy to use and is totally self-contained. The Piezo-Electric igniter eliminates the need for matches. This stove can be used both indoors and outdoors.

CAUTION: The stove is not a heater and should only be used for cooking. This stove is available at most Asian markets and can be purchased for less than $20.00. They can also be purchased in sporting goods stores and online for about $25.00 with shipping. Just search: "butane stove."

The butane canisters nestle into the side compartment of the stove and are also a bargain at the Asian Market. One canister will provide fuel for several meals depending on cook time. You would do well to practice with a few simple meals before putting your stove away for an emergency.

Each canister contains 220g of butane. The stove has a maximum rating of 7,650 Btu/Hr. with a maximum fuel consumption on high of 160g/hr. The heat output of this stove is roughly equal to the large burner on high of most electric ranges. One canister should then last about 1.25 hours on high and butane will store indefinitely. The Asian market I go to sells the fuel at four canisters for $5.00. That breaks down to $1.25 per canister.

One morning I used this stove to make pancakes and scrambled eggs in my kitchen. This was a breakfast for four. When I finished I weighed the canister to determine my fuel usage. The morning meal consumed slightly less than 50g of fuel. With 220g per canister that meant that I used about 20% of a canister. Cooking the same 20 minutes for each meal would mean that you would be able to cook at least five meals with one canister. If you just boil water for noodles or heat a can of soup or stew, you will use less fuel and the canister will last even longer.

AUTHOR'S ADVICE: Have 2 alternate cooking sources with adequate fuel available in your preparedness pantry.

Sprouting

Here is an amazing way to have fresh vegetables for your salad! Learn how to grow your own sprouts. Follow this process and you can have fresh sprouts on a regular basis.

Choose a handful of sprouts that you like. Not all sprouts are created equal! Once again I urge you to become familiar with this process, use sprouts from time to time in your menus. This is about as easy as it gets! Just a mason jar and some seeds is all it takes and you can sprout seeds.

I can recommend Alfalfa seeds, Clover seeds, Radish seeds, Broccoli seeds, Wheat seeds and Pea seeds. This is a well-rounded selection of seeds and you can make a very nutritious sprout salad. These seeds are easy to obtain, easy to sprout and are very agreeable. In time of crisis and you need fresh vegetables, sprouts can be an inexpensive answer. Plus they are very easy to sprout with the ability to add great taste to any meal.

Go to the health food store and buy a small amount of sprouts with the thought in mind that you will sprout and use them to be certain that you can do it and that you will eat them. The process is very simple and basically is the same for all sprouts. Be sure you purchase seeds that are for sprouting as garden seeds may be chemically treated.

A quart mason jar is an ideal sprouting container. You will need a lid that water can drain through. A nylon stocking is excellent, a piece of netting or even a piece of cheesecloth will make an excellent drain cap.

Follow These Three Simple Steps:

Step 1 – Soak Overnight

Place a total of 2 Tablespoons of seeds, mixed or individual in a one-quart Mason jar. Use the ring to attach *Sprouting Screen*. Cover with three times water. Let seeds soak 8-12 hours then pour water off. Peas, lentils and wheat use 1/2 to 3/4 cup of seeds.

Step 2 - Rinse 2 times a day

Rinse twice daily by covering the sprouts with water. Gently swirl water in jar. Drain off all the water after 5-10 minutes. This is just like watering your garden. Repeat this rinse two times each day for 4-6 days. There is no need to expose to direct sunlight. (Peas, lentils, wheat)*

Step 3 - De-hull in final rinse

Once you are ready to harvest, place all the sprouts in a bowl of water and gently agitate and separate sprouts and hulls. Let sprouts sit in sunlight for 8-10 hours to chlorophyll-up. The leaves will turn a rich green and increase in nutrition.

Enjoy! And keep your sprouts refrigerated!

114

Sprouts will last up to two weeks if well drained and stored in the refrigerator. Add peas, lentils and wheat to strews and soups. Use sprouts to garnish salads, sandwiches or just eat straight.

ENJOY!--- Endless Uses --- Excellent Nutrition --- Fresh Vegetables!

Sprouting Chart

Seeds	Seeds In Quart Jar	Soaking Time	Days To Harvest	Notes
Wheat*	1 Cup	8-12 Hrs.	2	Harvest when sprout is ½ the length
Alfalfa	2 Tbls.	8-12 Hrs.	6-7	Exposed to sunlight for the last day
Broccoli	2 Tbls.	8-12 Hrs.	6-7	Exposed to sunlight for the last day
Radish	2 Tbls.	8-12 Hrs.	6-7	Exposed to sunlight for the last day
Clover	2 Tbls.	8-12 Hrs.	6-7	Exposed to sunlight for the last day
Peas*	1 Cup	8-12 Hrs.	4	Harvest when 1/3 length of seed

Peas and wheat should sprout until sprout is about 1/3 the length of the seed.

Some Sprouting Hints:

For best flavor and nutrition use your sprouts within one week.

Keep harvested sprouts refrigerated.

Sprouts are an excellent source of vitamin C.

Green leafy sprouts filled with chlorophyll are a good source of vitamin A.

Sprouts are easy to digest.

Sprouts are low in calories and high in fiber.

Sprouts can be used in breads, soups, pancakes, omelets, casseroles, meatloaf, salads, or just eaten straight. They can also be used in smoothies and other nutritional drinks. Sprouts are excellent in place of lettuce on a sandwich.

Sprouting is one of nature's best kept secrets, a preparedness pantry with sprouts will always have healthy options. There is much written about sprouting and you may choose to expand your knowledge this section is intended to give you some basics with a well-rounded inventory of seeds. The most important thing here is to have a working knowledge and enough seed varieties that you will be able to add health and nutrition to your diet. Sprouting is something that you can add to your everyday diet.

Stackable spouting trays are an easy choice and are commercially available to make sprouting compact and efficient. I have found the Victorio 4 tray sprouting set to be excellent for all my sprouting. An added benefit is that the sprouts can store in the refrigerator and be served in the trays.

Photo Courtesy
www.victorio.info

The best part about sprouting is that is very easy and it can be done without the need of expensive special equipment.

Vegetables

There are several options for vegetables in your preparedness pantry. Probably the easiest option is to buy canned vegetables at your grocery store. Often you will find that seasonally your store will have a case lot sale this is a great time to stock up. If you are brave you might ask the store manager to give you a special price on cases of vegetables or other food products that you might buy in bulk. It doesn't hurt to ask and you just might hear "yes!"

You will need to decide which vegetables are best for you, obviously, this should be based on the vegetables that you eat on a regular basis. You may choose to have some frozen and some caned. You may also have dried vegetables from your garden. This actually is an excellent way to build your preparedness pantry. In fact, you can provide a large portion of your fruits and vegetables from your own garden by drying and canning your produce. We will not cover drying or canning in this book however, personally 75% of the vegetables I eat out of season were dried or canned from my own 1500 square foot garden.

Once again we will use the same process to determine needs. Choose the vegetables that you will use in your preparedness pantry. Then determine how many times your family will eat that particular vegetable in a one-year period. If your family uses only one can per meal then it is very simple, if you are to eat that particular vegetable once a week then you will need to have 52 cans of that vegetable in your preparedness pantry in rotation. If you eat one half of a can then divide 52 by 2 and place 26 cans in your preparedness pantry.

Here is a partial list of some canned vegetables to consider:

• Beans	• Peas	• _____
• Beets	• Spinach	• _____
• Carrots	• Tomato paste	• _____
• Corn	• Tomato sauce	• _____
• Olives	• Tomatoes	• _____

Add to this list to complete your vegetable inventory in your preparedness pantry.

Once you have chosen the vegetables you will have in your preparedness pantry determine the quantities that you need to have in rotation and add them to the grand total table. Don't forget to consider that you may also want to include some of these vegetables in your lunch menu.

If you choose to have canned product in your preparedness pantry it is imperative that you rotate your storage I cannot emphasize this enough.

Dehydrated Vegetables

Dehydrated vegetables are probably the best option available for the preparedness pantry. Stored properly dried vegetables will last 10 or more years. This makes them an excellent option. You can learn to dry your own fruits and vegetables and add to your preparedness pantry every year a large amount of produce much of it coming from your garden. Buying on sales or even using the surplus produce of your neighbors and friends.

This is a simple process, though we do not have time in this book to cover I refer you to my book *Drying Fruits And Vegetables Made Easy*, available at www.samspencer.us and the 2 DVD companion set that is also available to teach and demonstrate the art of drying fruits and vegetables. You can also purchase dried vegetables in #10 cans, cook them as per the instructions on the can to fill your vegetable needs.

You can mix and cook these vegetables in a vegetable stew or soup. You can serve them as a single serving or you can mix them in a casserole. You can also purchase mixed vegetable stew and soup mixes to which you just add water. These will be a good options until you learn how to dry and store produce in your own dehydrators.

Powdered Products

Dried mixes can be an excellent preparedness pantry items. They will last many years in their sealed container and can be interchanged for dried. For example: 2 Tbls. of powdered milk can replace one cup of milk by adding just under 1 cup of water. Powdered butter, powdered shortening, powdered eggs and powdered cheese can be used in most recipes on a one to one exchange.

Learn how you can use powdered product in your everyday cooking to add greater convenience not to mention that you will already know how to use this product and it will be readily available in your preparedness pantry.

You'll be amazed at how many powdered products are available, you would also be amazed to know that much of it is used in the prepared products that you already purchase from the grocery store. You can even save some money by making your own prepared powdered additives.

Appendix C is a table that will help you in converting your recipes to be able to use powdered product. With powdered product you can prepare mixes in bulk that you can use by just adding water to simplify your daily meals. Breads, pancakes, muffins, and items like cornbread our mixes you can easily prepare this way.

Final Steps

The final step is to consolidate the *Total Volume Tables* into one grand table (Appendix C). This will give you the final totals completing the storage inventory that you will need to maintain. The most significant feature of this final table is that you now have a hard list of preparedness food supplies that is practical and well defined. This list will become the foundation for an exceptional preparedness pantry.

Now transfer the totals from the previous *Volume Tables* onto the *Grand Total Volume Tables* (Appendix C) this

will determine your final numbers.

Be sure to add to the final list extra ingredients for treats and personal favorites. This book is to teach you principals of an effective preparedness plan. With this knowledge you can add and subtract based on

your needs now knowing how to add product and how to figure your annual needs.

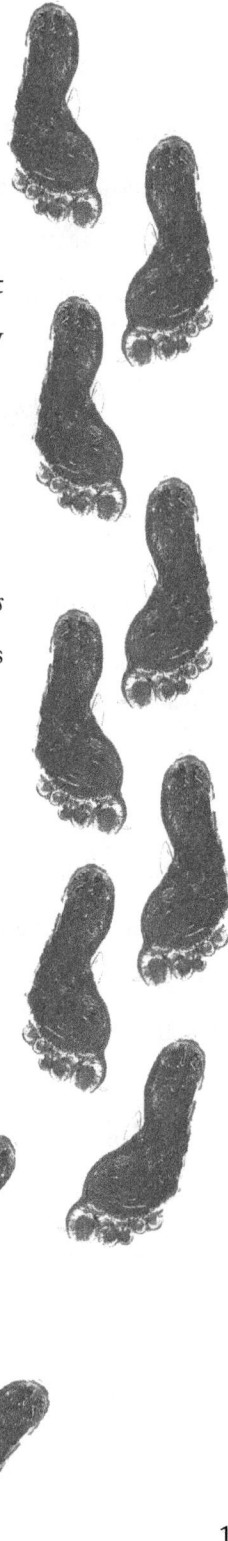

Grand Finale

Now that you have completed the organization step in implementing a preparedness pantry program, it is time to start the acquisition step. The money available will largely dictate this. It will generally take significant sacrifice to complete this step so it is important to start in chunks that you can handle. If you put together a plan to follow your chances of success will be much better, the biggest challenge will be following your plan.

If you have sufficient resources then jump right in! Otherwise determine how much you can commit to this project each month. The amount of importance you attach to building a preparedness pantry program will be proportional to the effort you put into accomplishing it.

I have a couple of perspectives to share with you. Once you have determined how much money and time you are willing to dedicate to completing this project, simply start at the top and begin to purchase the your preparedness pantry items like grains, powdered items and sugar. Then fill in the gaps as you go. Set a goal as to when you would like to have this project complete and track your progress.

Another idea would be to take all the needs and built them one fourth at a time. Divide the needs by 4 and build your storage in 90 day increments. 91 days is 1/4 of 365 days. If a 90 day increment is to hard then use a 30 day plan and divide the total by 10 and work from there.

If you are just starting out, or have limited space or resources, first fill out the complete plan for a year's supply in your preparedness pantry. This means that you try-out the various recipes and add additional recipes as desired. Next divide the total by 10 and you will have a five week supply. Purchase the complete inventory for a five week preparedness pantry. What a great accomplishment!

The next step is to do it again which will bring you to 60 days worth of food in your preparedness pantry. One more time will give you 90 days. Building as you can is critical to ultimate success. The most important thing is to be working on the project faithfully and continually. There will be roadblocks placed in the way and that's life. The challenge is to take the detour without losing focus on the ultimate goal!

So let's get started, go out today and buy something to get you started, then go out tomorrow and get something else. Just keep getting a few items each time you go to the store, order the long-term items that you need. Commit to do something regularly to complete this task!

GOOD LUCK!

A Word About Rotation

We can get all caught up in rotating our food yet if we use this simple menu system that I have taught you rotation can become quite easy! Once you have completed your master inventory or appendix C you will simply need to take an inventory once a month. Total all that you have in your preparedness pantry. Once you have the inventory totals, simple purchase what you need to bring your inventory up to the proper levels.

Prepare one breakfast, one lunch and one dinner from your preparedness pantry menu each week and every 7 years you auto rotate your food. Prepare two breakfasts, two lunches and two dinners from your preparedness pantry menu each week and every 3 ½ years you auto rotate your food. Prepare three breakfasts, three lunches and three dinners from your preparedness pantry menu each week and slightly over every year and a half you will auto rotate your food this is why it is very important to center your food storage around the menus that you eat today. Store what you eat and eat what you store.

Take time to complete all the worksheets to organize your food storage and food storage will be easy!

Some Closing Thoughts

Now that you have read this whole book you are probably overwhelmed and wonder where do I start? How can I work it in? Here is a suggested plan to follow to begin to implement this program.

Week One:

Study the entire book to catch the vision. Study it with your spouse and family to get all onboard that you can.

Week Two:

Try out the breakfast recipes and determine which ones will be in your preparedness menu and how many of the 365 breakfasts you will incorporate in your meal plan. Tally and add the totals to your inventory sheet.

Week Three:

Try out the lunch and bread recipes and determine which ones will be in your preparedness menu and how many times in 365 days you will prepare each recipe. Tally and add the totals to your inventory sheet.

Week Four:

Try out the lunch and bread recipes and determine which ones will be in your preparedness menu and how many times in 365 days you will prepare each recipe. Tally and add the totals to your inventory sheet.

You will now have a complete inventory of what you need to purchase for your preparedness pantry. Remember that this is what you need to maintain in your preparedness pantry, or maybe it is better said that this is the level that you need to build toward.

Week Five:

Get everyone together and review the inventory to formulate a plan that will fill your preparedness pantry. Now you need to start filling the pantry.

Some Advice:

You have a huge project here. You are actually trying to plan for several thousand meals, like the chef on a cruise ship. It will take some time and continued management. With this task appearing so enormous, we need to cut it into bite size pieces. If you have the resources to just go down your list and fill your pantry at once that is great, get it done! If 365 days is too much then divide the total inventory totals by 4 and purchase in "90 day supply" increments. Once you complete this process you will be done!

If 90 days is still too much that is okay, do not fret, you have a total that you need to work toward so divide the total by 10 and start with a 5 week supply. The most important thing is to be actively working consistently on this project. If you focus on this project you will complete it in time, just do it before it is too late!

So raise your right hand and repeat: "I promise myself to stock-up a little extra product in my preparedness pantry each week."

Now go make yourself proud!

APPENDIX

Appendix A

Worksheet to add to Appendix C

Canned Fruits

Ingredients	Breakfast			Lunch			Dinner												Grad Total		
	t	T	C	t	T	C	t	T	C	t	T	C	t	T	C	t	T	C	t	T	C
Applesauce																					
Fruit Cocktail																					
Mandarin Oranges																					
Peaches																					
Pears																					
Pineapple																					

Appendix A

Worksheet to add to Appendix C

Canned Vegetables

Ingredients	Breakfast			Lunch			Dinner												Grad Total		
Beans	t	T	c	t	T	c	t	T	c	t	T	c	t	T	c	t	T	c	t	T	c
Beets	t	T	c	t	T	c	t	T	c	t	T	c	t	T	c	t	T	c	t	T	c
Carrots	t	T	c	t	T	c	t	T	c	t	T	c	t	T	c	t	T	c	t	T	c
Corn	t	T	c	t	T	c	t	T	c	t	T	c	t	T	c	t	T	c	t	T	c
Olives	t	T	c	t	T	c	t	T	c	t	T	c	t	T	c	t	T	c	t	T	c
Peas	t	T	c	t	T	c	t	T	c	t	T	c	t	T	c	t	T	c	t	T	c
Tomato Paste	t	T	c	t	T	c	t	T	c	t	T	c	t	T	c	t	T	c	t	T	c
Tomato Sauce	t	T	c	t	T	c	t	T	c	t	T	c	t	T	c	t	T	c	t	T	c
Tomatoes	t	T	c	t	T	c	t	T	c	t	T	c	t	T	c	t	T	c	t	T	c
	t	T	c	t	T	c	t	T	c	t	T	c	t	T	c	t	T	c	t	T	c
	t	T	c	t	T	c	t	T	c	t	T	c	t	T	c	t	T	c	t	T	c
	t	T	c	t	T	c	t	T	c	t	T	c	t	T	c	t	T	c	t	T	c
	t	T	c	t	T	c	t	T	c	t	T	c	t	T	c	t	T	c	t	T	c
	t	T	c	t	T	c	t	T	c	t	T	c	t	T	c	t	T	c	t	T	c
	t	T	c	t	T	c	t	T	c	t	T	c	t	T	c	t	T	c	t	T	c
	t	T	c	t	T	c	t	T	c	t	T	c	t	T	c	t	T	c	t	T	c

Appendix C

This worksheet will become the foundation for a comprehensive yet practical preparedness pantry. Fill it out the best you can. Add to it regularly. Fill and maintain in your preparedness pantry the volumes and quantities that you have estimated. Take a physical inventory monthly, fill in the gaps regularly, adjust as needed and use your pantry daily.

Preparedness Pantry Inventory Consolidated Worksheet

Mark "t" teaspoons, "T" Tablespoons or "C" cups above input number

#Preparations							
Ingredients	Breakfast	Lunch	Dinner	Appendix A	Appendix B	Other	Grad Total
Baking Powder	t T C	t T C	t T C	t T C	t T C	t T C	t T C
Baking Soda	t T C	t T C	t T C	t T C	t T C	t T C	t T C
Beans, Black	t T C	t T C	t T C	t T C	t T C	t T C	t T C
Beans, Pinto	t T C	t T C	t T C	t T C	t T C	t T C	t T C
Beans, Red Kidney	t T C	t T C	t T C	t T C	t T C	t T C	t T C
Beans, Refried	t T C	t T C	t T C	t T C	t T C	t T C	t T C
Beans, White	t T C	t T C	t T C	t T C	t T C	t T C	t T C
Bullion, Beef	t T C	t T C	t T C	t T C	t T C	t T C	t T C
Bullion, Chicken	t T C	t T C	t T C	t T C	t T C	t T C	t T C
Catsup	t T C	t T C	t T C	t T C	t T C	t T C	t T C
Chicken	t T C	t T C	t T C	t T C	t T C	t T C	t T C
Chocolate Chips	t T C	t T C	t T C	t T C	t T C	t T C	t T C
Chocolate Milk	t T C	t T C	t T C	t T C	t T C	t T C	t T C

Item	t	T	c	t	T	c	t	T	c	t	T	c	t	T	c	t	T	c	t	T	c
Cinnamon	t	T	c	t	T	c	t	T	c	t	T	c	t	T	c	t	T	c	t	T	c
Cold Cereal	t	T	c	t	T	c	t	T	c	t	T	c	t	T	c	t	T	c	t	T	c
Corn, Dent	t	T	c	t	T	c	t	T	c	t	T	c	t	T	c	t	T	c	t	T	c
Corn, Popping	t	T	c	t	T	c	t	T	c	t	T	c	t	T	c	t	T	c	t	T	c
Corn Starch	t	T	c	t	T	c	t	T	c	t	T	c	t	T	c	t	T	c	t	T	c
Flour, Baking	t	T	c	t	T	c	t	T	c	t	T	c	t	T	c	t	T	c	t	T	c
Honey	t	T	c	t	T	c	t	T	c	t	T	c	t	T	c	t	T	c	t	T	c
Jam/Jelly	t	T	c	t	T	c	t	T	c	t	T	c	t	T	c	t	T	c	t	T	c
Macaroni	t	T	c	t	T	c	t	T	c	t	T	c	t	T	c	t	T	c	t	T	c
Noodles	t	T	c	t	T	c	t	T	c	t	T	c	t	T	c	t	T	c	t	T	c
Nuts	t	T	c	t	T	c	t	T	c	t	T	c	t	T	c	t	T	c	t	T	c
Oatmeal, 3-minute	t	T	c	t	T	c	t	T	c	t	T	c	t	T	c	t	T	c	t	T	c
Oatmeal, Instant	t	T	c	t	T	c	t	T	c	t	T	c	t	T	c	t	T	c	t	T	c
Peanut Butter	t	T	c	t	T	c	t	T	c	t	T	c	t	T	c	t	T	c	t	T	c
Pearled Barley	t	T	c	t	T	c	t	T	c	t	T	c	t	T	c	t	T	c	t	T	c
Pork And Beans	t	T	c	t	T	c	t	T	c	t	T	c	t	T	c	t	T	c	t	T	c
Potatoes, Flakes	t	T	c	t	T	c	t	T	c	t	T	c	t	T	c	t	T	c	t	T	c
Potatoes, Granules	t	T	c	t	T	c	t	T	c	t	T	c	t	T	c	t	T	c	t	T	c
Potatoes, Pearls	t	T	c	t	T	c	t	T	c	t	T	c	t	T	c	t	T	c	t	T	c
Raisins	t	T	c	t	T	c	t	T	c	t	T	c	t	T	c	t	T	c	t	T	c
Raman Noodle	t	T	c	t	T	c	t	T	c	t	T	c	t	T	c	t	T	c	t	T	c

	t	T	C	t	T	C	t	T	C	t	T	C	t	T	C	t	T	C	t	T	C
Rice, Brown																						
Rice, Jasmine																						
Rice, Minute																						
Rice, Parboiled																						
Salsa																						
Salt																						
Soup, Cream Of Celery																						
Soup, Cream of Chicken																						
Soup, Cream of Mushroom																						
Soup, Tomato																						
Spaghetti																						
Sugar, Brown																						
Sugar, Granulated																						
Syrup, Maple																						
Syrup, Corn																						
Tuna Fish																						
Wheat, Flour																						
Wheat, Storage																						
Yeast, Dried																						

	t	T	C	t	T	C	t	T	C	t	T	C	t	T	C	t	T	C	t	T	C
	t	T	C	t	T	C	t	T	C	t	T	C	t	T	C	t	T	C	t	T	C
	t	T	C	t	T	C	t	T	C	t	T	C	t	T	C	t	T	C	t	T	C
	t	T	C	t	T	C	t	T	C	t	T	C	t	T	C	t	T	C	t	T	C
	t	T	C	t	T	C	t	T	C	t	T	C	t	T	C	t	T	C	t	T	C
	t	T	C	t	T	C	t	T	C	t	T	C	t	T	C	t	T	C	t	T	C
	t	T	C	t	T	C	t	T	C	t	T	C	t	T	C	t	T	C	t	T	C
	t	T	C	t	T	C	t	T	C	t	T	C	t	T	C	t	T	C	t	T	C
	t	T	C	t	T	C	t	T	C	t	T	C	t	T	C	t	T	C	t	T	C
	t	T	C	t	T	C	t	T	C	t	T	C	t	T	C	t	T	C	t	T	C
	t	T	C	t	T	C	t	T	C	t	T	C	t	T	C	t	T	C	t	T	C
	t	T	C	t	T	C	t	T	C	t	T	C	t	T	C	t	T	C	t	T	C
	t	T	C	t	T	C	t	T	C	t	T	C	t	T	C	t	T	C	t	T	C
	t	T	C	t	T	C	t	T	C	t	T	C	t	T	C	t	T	C	t	T	C
	t	T	C	t	T	C	t	T	C	t	T	C	t	T	C	t	T	C	t	T	C
	t	T	C	t	T	C	t	T	C	t	T	C	t	T	C	t	T	C	t	T	C
	t	T	C	t	T	C	t	T	C	t	T	C	t	T	C	t	T	C	t	T	C
	t	T	C	t	T	C	t	T	C	t	T	C	t	T	C	t	T	C	t	T	C
	t	T	C	t	T	C	t	T	C	t	T	C	t	T	C	t	T	C	t	T	C
	t	T	C	t	T	C	t	T	C	t	T	C	t	T	C	t	T	C	t	T	C
	t	T	C	t	T	C	t	T	C	t	T	C	t	T	C	t	T	C	t	T	C

Vegetables Dried

Ingredients																						Grad Total	
	t	T	C	t	T	C	t	T	C	t	T	C	t	T	C	t	T	C	t	T	C	t	T	C
Beans																								
Broccoli	t	T	C	t	T	C	t	T	C	t	T	C	t	T	C	t	T	C	t	T	C
Carrots	t	T	C	t	T	C	t	T	C	t	T	C	t	T	C	t	T	C	t	T	C
Celery	t	T	C	t	T	C	t	T	C	t	T	C	t	T	C	t	T	C	t	T	C
Corn	t	T	C	t	T	C	t	T	C	t	T	C	t	T	C	t	T	C	t	T	C
Peas	t	T	C	t	T	C	t	T	C	t	T	C	t	T	C	t	T	C	t	T	C
Tomatoes	t	T	C	t	T	C	t	T	C	t	T	C	t	T	C	t	T	C	t	T	C
	t	T	C	t	T	C	t	T	C	t	T	C	t	T	C	t	T	C	t	T	C
	t	T	C	t	T	C	t	T	C	t	T	C	t	T	C	t	T	C	t	T	C
	t	T	C	t	T	C	t	T	C	t	T	C	t	T	C	t	T	C	t	T	C
	t	T	C	t	T	C	t	T	C	t	T	C	t	T	C	t	T	C	t	T	C
	t	T	C	t	T	C	t	T	C	t	T	C	t	T	C	t	T	C	t	T	C
	t	T	C	t	T	C	t	T	C	t	T	C	t	T	C	t	T	C	t	T	C
	t	T	C	t	T	C	t	T	C	t	T	C	t	T	C	t	T	C	t	T	C

Dried / Powder Product

Ingredients																						Grad Total	
	t	T	C	t	T	C	t	T	C	t	T	C	t	T	C	t	T	C	t	T	C	t	T	C
Bananas																								
Shortening/ Oil Powder	t	T	C	t	T	C	t	T	C	t	T	C	t	T	C	t	T	C	t	T	C
Margarine Powder	t	T	C	t	T	C	t	T	C	t	T	C	t	T	C	t	T	C	t	T	C

Ingredients	t	T	C	t	T	C	t	T	C	t	T	C	t	T	C	t	T	C	t	T	C	t	T	C
Milk Powder																								
Butter Powder																								
Eggs Powder																								
Cheese Powder																								
Buttermilk Powder																								
Apples, Dried																								
Soup Mix																								

Canned Vegetables

Ingredients																							Grad Total
Beans	t	T	C	t	T	C	t	T	C	t	T	C	t	T	C	t	T	C	t	T	C	t	T	C
Beets	t	T	C	t	T	C	t	T	C	t	T	C	t	T	C	t	T	C	t	T	C	t	T	C
Carrots	t	T	C	t	T	C	t	T	C	t	T	C	t	T	C	t	T	C	t	T	C	t	T	C
Corn	t	T	C	t	T	C	t	T	C	t	T	C	t	T	C	t	T	C	t	T	C	t	T	C
Olives	t	T	C	t	T	C	t	T	C	t	T	C	t	T	C	t	T	C	t	T	C	t	T	C
Peas	t	T	C	t	T	C	t	T	C	t	T	C	t	T	C	t	T	C	t	T	C	t	T	C
Tomato Paste	t	T	C	t	T	C	t	T	C	t	T	C	t	T	C	t	T	C	t	T	C	t	T	C
Tomato Sauce	t	T	C	t	T	C	t	T	C	t	T	C	t	T	C	t	T	C	t	T	C	t	T	C
Tomatoes	t	T	C	t	T	C	t	T	C	t	T	C	t	T	C	t	T	C	t	T	C	t	T	C

	t	T	C	t	T	C	t	T	C	t	T	C	t	T	C	t	T	C	t	T	C
	t	T	C	t	T	C	t	T	C	t	T	C	t	T	C	t	T	C	t	T	C
	t	T	C	t	T	C	t	T	C	t	T	C	t	T	C	t	T	C	t	T	C
	t	T	C	t	T	C	t	T	C	t	T	C	t	T	C	t	T	C	t	T	C
	t	T	C	t	T	C	t	T	C	t	T	C	t	T	C	t	T	C	t	T	C
	t	T	C	t	T	C	t	T	C	t	T	C	t	T	C	t	T	C	t	T	C
	t	T	C	t	T	C	t	T	C	t	T	C	t	T	C	t	T	C	t	T	C

Vegetables Dried

Ingredients							Grad Total
Beans	t T C	t T C	t T C	t T C	t T C	t T C	t T C
Broccoli	t T C	t T C	t T C	t T C	t T C	t T C	t T C
Carrots	t T C	t T C	t T C	t T C	t T C	t T C	t T C
Celery	t T C	t T C	t T C	t T C	t T C	t T C	t T C
Corn	t T C	t T C	t T C	t T C	t T C	t T C	t T C
Peas	t T C	t T C	t T C	t T C	t T C	t T C	t T C
Tomatoes	t T C	t T C	t T C	t T C	t T C	t T C	t T C
	t T C	t T C	t T C	t T C	t T C	t T C	t T C
	t T C	t T C	t T C	t T C	t T C	t T C	t T C
	t T C	t T C	t T C	t T C	t T C	t T C	t T C
	t T C	t T C	t T C	t T C	t T C	t T C	t T C
	t T C	t T C	t T C	t T C	t T C	t T C	t T C

Seasonings

Ingredient	t	T	C	t	T	C	t	T	C	t	T	C	t	T	C	t	T	C	t	T	C
Basil																					
Cinnamon																					
Italian Seasoning Mix																					
Lemon Pepper																					
Onion																					
Oregano																					
Pepper																					

Sprouting Seeds

Ingredients	t	T	C	t	T	C	t	T	C	t	T	C	t	T	C	t	T	C	Grad Total t	T	C
Alfalfa																					
Broccoli																					
Clover																					
Peas																					
Radish																					
Wheat																					

Other Items

Ingredients								Grad Total
Condensed Milk	t T C	t T C	t T C	t T C	t T C	t T C	t T C	
Crackers	t T C	t T C	t T C	t T C	t T C	t T C	t T C	
Cream of Tarter	t T C	t T C	t T C	t T C	t T C	t T C	t T C	
Evaporated Milk	t T C	t T C	t T C	t T C	t T C	t T C	t T C	
Salad Dressing	t T C	t T C	t T C	t T C	t T C	t T C	t T C	
	t T C	t T C	t T C	t T C	t T C	t T C	t T C	
	t T C	t T C	t T C	t T C	t T C	t T C	t T C	
	t T C	t T C	t T C	t T C	t T C	t T C	t T C	

Canned Fruits

Ingredients								Grad Total
Applesauce	t T C	t T C	t T C	t T C	t T C	t T C	t T C	
Fruit Cocktail	t T C	t T C	t T C	t T C	t T C	t T C	t T C	
Mandarin Oranges	t T C	t T C	t T C	t T C	t T C	t T C	t T C	
Peaches	t T C	t T C	t T C	t T C	t T C	t T C	t T C	
Pears	t T C	t T C	t T C	t T C	t T C	t T C	t T C	
Pineapple	t T C	t T C	t T C	t T C	t T C	t T C	t T C	
	t T C	t T C	t T C	t T C	t T C	t T C	t T C	
	t T C	t T C	t T C	t T C	t T C	t T C	t T C	

Appendix D

Universal Volume Calculation Table

The following table can be used to determine the volume needed in a recipe. It works equally well both for Tablespoons and for cups since there are 16 Tablespoons in a cup and there are 16 Cups in a gallon. Therefore if you start in Tablespoons the answer will be cups and if you start in cups the answer will be in gallons.

In the far left column you have the numbers 1 through 12 representing the number of Tablespoons or Cups needed for the recipe. Across the top, in increments of 50, is the number of preparations that you would like to add to your preparedness pantry. If your family size requires that you increase a recipe you will also need to multiply either one of the two numbers by that same factor. In other words if your recipe calls for 2 Tablespoons and you will double the recipe for your size of family then you must double the 2 Tablespoons to 4 or you will need to double the number of preparations in the top row which is 50 to 100. You will only increase one of the numbers by the recipe size factor you are using. (double x 2, triple x 3)

Example:

4 Tbls. X 150 preparations = 37 1/2 Cups for your preparedness pantry. This is the total cups that you need to add to your preparedness pantry. I you choose to divide that number by 16 you will also have the number of gallons.

The same calculation method works if your recipe calls for Cups:
4 Cups X 150 preparations = 37 1/2 Gallons for your preparedness pantry. This is the total gallons that you need to add to your preparedness pantry.

Repeat this step for each ingredient in your recipe to figure the quantity you need to store in your preparedness pantry.

Please note that Tablespoons will yield cups and the cups will yield gallons.

The number at the intersection is the number of cups or gallons that you will need. If you are using Tablespoons the number at the intersection is cups if you are using cups the number at the intersection will be gallons.

By using this table you will be able to quickly determine the approximate volume you will need to add to your preparedness pantry. Use it for all your calculations. Round up where needed, it is better to have a little extra than to wish you had more! Besides you will have something to share or a product of value with which to barter!

Tablespoon / Cups Conversion Table

Total Number Of Preparations Needed (Tablespoons will yield Cups, Cups will yield Gallons)								
		50	100	150	200	250	300	350	400
Number Of Tablespoons Or Cups In Recipe	1	3 1/8	6 1/4	9 3/8	12 1/2	15 5/8	18 3/4	21 7/8	25
	2	6 1/4	12 1/2	18 3/4	25	31 1/4	37 1/2	43 3/4	50
	3	9 3/8	18 3/4	28 1/8	37 1/2	46 7/8	56 1/4	65 5/8	75
	4	12 1/2	25	37 1/2	50	62 1/2	75	87 1/2	100
	5	15 5/8	31 1/4	46 7/8	62 1/2	78 1/8	93 3/4	109 3/8	125
	6	18 3/4	37 1/2	56 1/4	75	93 3/4	112 1/2	131 1/4	150
	7	21 7/8	43 3/4	65 5/8	87 1/2	109 3/8	131 1/4	153 1/8	175
	8	25	50	75	100	125	150	175	200
	9	28 1/8	56 1/4	84 3/8	112 1/2	140 5/8	168 3/4	196 7/8	225
	10	31 1/4	62 1/2	93 3/4	125	156 1/4	187 1/2	218 3/4	250
	11	34 3/8	68 3/4	103 1/8	137 1/2	171 7/8	206 1/4	240 5/8	275
	12	37 1/2	75	112 1/2	150	187 1/2	225	262 1/2	300

©2012 Sam Spencer

For those who like to skip around, this table is more easily understood when you have read this book and understand the preparedness pantry concept.

teaspoon Conversion Table

		Total Number Of Preparations Needed (teaspoons will yield Cups)							
		50	100	150	200	250	300	350	400
Number Of teaspoons In Recipe	1	1	2	3 1/8	4 1/6	5 1/5	6 1/4	7 2/7	8 1/3
	2	2	4 1/6	6 1/4	8 1/3	10 2/5	12 1/2	14 3/5	16 2/3
	3	3 1/8	6 1/4	9 3/8	12 1/2	15 5/8	18 3/4	21 7/8	25
	4	4 1/6	8 1/3	12 1/2	16 2/3	20 5/6	25	29 1/6	33 1/3
	5	5 1/5	10 3/7	15 5/8	20 5/6	26	31 1/4	36 1/2	41 2/3
	6	6 1/4	12 1/2	18 3/4	25	31 1/4	37 1/2	43 3/4	50
	7	21 7/8	43 3/4	65 5/8	87 1/2	109 3/8	131 1/4	153 1/8	175
	8	8 1/3	16 2/3	25	33 1/3	41 2/3	50	58 1/3	66 2/3
	9	9 3/8	18 3/4	28 1/8	37 1/2	46 7/8	56 1/4	65 5/8	75
	10	10 3/7	20 5/6	31 1/4	41 2/3	52	62 1/2	73	83 1/3
	11	11 1/2	23	34 3/8	45 5/6	57 2/7	68 3/4	80 1/5	91 2/3
	12	12 1/2	25	37 1/2	50	62 1/2	75	87 1/2	100

©2012 Sam Spencer

Appendix E

Dry Ingredients Conversion Table

Powdered	Mix Ratio	Powder	Water	Makes
Milk	1:8	2 Tbsp.	7/8 cup	1 Cup
Condensed Milk	1:4	4 Tbsp.	3/4 Cup	1 Cup
Butter	1:1	1 Tbsp.	1 Tbsp.	2 Tbsp.
Cheese	1:2	1 Tbsp.	2 Tbsp.	3 Tbsp.
Eggs	1:1	2 Tbsp.	2 Tbsp.	1 Egg
Egg Whites	1:1	2 Tbsp.	2 Tbsp.	1 Egg
Margarine	1:1	1 Tbsp.	1 Tbsp.	2 Tbsp.
Shortening	1:1	1 Tbsp.	1 Tbsp.	2 Tbsp.

To use the above chart you simply add the Tablespoons of dry powder to your recipe plus the appropriate amount the additional liquid. It is that simple! Experiment with your dried powders and soon you will be using them all the time.

Appendix F

Sample Worksheet

Breakfast Menu Total Volume Table

Mark "t" teaspoons, "T" Tablespoons or "C" cups above input number

#Preparations	150			50			50			50			50						Grad Total		
Ingredients	Pancakes			Muffins			Oatmeal			Wheat			Eggs								
	t	T	C	t	T	C	t	T	C	t	T	C	t	T	C	t	T	C	t	T	C
Apples, Dried																					
Applesauce						*15*															*15*
Baking Powder	*300*			*100*															*400*		
Baking Soda																					
Bananas, Dried						*25*															*25*
Butter, Powdered														*50*						*50*	
Catsup																					
Chocolate Chips																					
Chocolate Milk																					
Cinnamon																					
Cold Cereal																					
Eggs, Powdered		*300*			*100*															*400*	
Flour, Baking																					

Script Indicates Your Calculations

Item	t	T	c	t	T	c	t	T	c	t	T	c	t	T	c	t	T	c	t	T	c	t	T	c
Honey																								
Jam/Jelly																								
Margarine, Powdered																								
Milk, Powdered		600			150						100			100									950	
Nuts																								
Oatmeal, 3-minute																								
Oatmeal, Instant						100																		100
Raisins					50																		50	
Salsa																								
Salt	75			25																		100		
Shortening/ Oil, Powdered		300				17																		36
Sugar, Brown		450				17		100																52
Sugar, Granulated																								
Syrup																								
Wheat, Flour																								
Wheat, Storage			150			75						100			50									375
Yeast, Dried																								

Divide Total teaspoons by 48 to convert to Cups

Divide Total Tablespoons by 16 to convert to Cups

Divide Total Cups by 16 to convert to Gallons

Appendix G

There can be an endless list of items that can be put in your preparedness pantry. Below is a partial list of a few items that you should consider as you build your pantry. Add to and delete from the list based on your needs. Most important is to begin to think of how you will prepare food with limited resources.

Here are a few suggested hardware items for your preparedness pantry:

☐ Blender

☐ Mill for grinding grains

☐ Hand powered mill

☐ Small Generator

☐ 25' heavy duty extension cord

☐ Hand powered Egg Beater

☐ Solar Oven

☐ Camp Stove

☐ Dutch oven

☐ Matches

☐ Fire Starter

☐ Water containers

☐ Charcoal

☐ Gas Grill

☐ Extra bottle of gas

☐ _____

☐ _____

☐ _____

☐ _____

☐ _____

☐ _____

☐ _____

☐ _____

☐ _____

Check off the ones you like and line out the ones that do not fit. As you prepare your preparations make sure that you have the proper cooking hardware in your preparedness pantry.

Add additional items that fit into your preparedness plan.

HAVE FUN!

Appendix H

Recipe Calculator

Use this worksheet to help organize your recipes and extend the totals to the **Preparedness Pantry Inventory Consolidated Worksheet. (**Appendix C**)**

___150___ Number Preparations   ___Whole Wheat Pancakes___ Recipe

Volume	Ingredient	# Preparations	Total Needed	Total Needed
__1__ Cups	__Wheat__ X	__150__ =	__150__ ÷ 16 =	__9.375__ Gallons
__2__ Tbls	__P. Eggs__ X	__150__ =	__300__ ÷ 16 =	__18.75__ Cups
__3__ Tbls	__P. Milk__ X	__150__ =	__450__ ÷ 16 =	__28.125__ Cups
__3__ Tbls	__Sugar__ X	__150__ =	__450__ ÷ 16 =	__28.125__ Cups
__2__ Tbls	__P. Butter__ X	__150__ =	__300__ ÷ 16 =	__18.75__ Cups
__2__ tsps.	__B Powder__ X	__150__ =	__300__ ÷ 48 =	__6.25__ Cups
__1/2__ tsps.	__Salt__ X	__150__ =	__75__ ÷ 48 =	__1.5__ Cups

©2012 Sam Spencer

Appendix H

Recipe Calculator

Use this worksheet to help organize your recipes and extend the totals to the **Preparedness Pantry Inventory Consolidated Worksheet.** (Appendix C)

__185__ Number Of Preparations __Whole Wheat Bread__ Recipe

Volume	Ingredient	# Preparations	Total Needed	Total Needed	
_4_ Cups	_Wheat Flour_	X _185_	= _740_	÷ 16 = _46.25_	Gallons
_1/3_Cups	_Brown Sugar_	X _185_	= _62_	÷ 16 = _3.9_	Gallons
___ Cups	_____	X _____	= _____	÷ 16 = _____	Gallons
___ Cups	_____	X _____	= _____	÷ 16 = _____	Gallons
_2_ Tbls.	_Pdr. Milk_	X _185_	= _370_	÷ 16 = _23.25_	Cups
_2_ Tbls.	_Pdr. Butter_	X _185_	= _370_	÷ 16 = _23.25_	Cups
___ Tbls.	_____	X _____	= _____	÷ 16 = _____	Cups
___ Tbls.	_____	X _____	= _____	÷ 16 = _____	Cups
_2_ tsps.	_Salt_	X _185_	= _370_	÷ 48 = _7.75_	Cups
_2_ tsps.	_Yeast_	X _185_	= _370_	÷ 48 = _7.75_	Cups
___ tsps.	_____	X _____	= _____	÷ 48 = _____	Cups
___ tsps.	_____	X _____	= _____	÷ 48 = _____	Cups

Other Ingredients:

___ _____	_____ X _____	=	_____
___ _____	_____ X _____	=	_____
___ _____	_____ X _____	=	_____

Appendix H

Recipe Calculator

Use this worksheet to help organize your recipes and extend the totals to the **Preparedness Pantry Inventory Consolidated Worksheet.** (Appendix C)

_75_ Number Of Preparations _Tuna & Rice Casserole_ Recipe

Volume	Ingredient		# Preparations	Total Needed		Total Needed	

_1_ Cups _Brown Rice_ X _75_ = _75_ ÷ 16 = _4.25_ Gallons

___ Cups _____ X _____ = _____ ÷ 16 = _____ Gallons

___ Cups _____ X _____ = _____ ÷ 16 = _____ Gallons

___ Cups _____ X _____ = _____ ÷ 16 = _____ Gallons

_1_ Tbls. _Pdr. Milk_ X _75_ = _75_ ÷ 16 = _4.25_ Cups

___ Tbls. _____ X _____ = _____ ÷ 16 = _____ Cups

___ Tbls. _____ X _____ = _____ ÷ 16 = _____ Cups

___ tsps. _____ X _____ = _____ ÷ 48 = _____ Cups

___ tsps. _____ X _____ = _____ ÷ 48 = _____ Cups

___ tsps. _____ X _____ = _____ ÷ 48 = _____ Cups

___ tsps. _____ X _____ = _____ ÷ 48 = _____ Cups

Other Ingredients:

_1_ _Can_ _Tuna_ X _75_ = _75_

_1_ _Can_ _Peas_ X _75_ = _75_

_1_ _Can_ _Cream Of Mushroom_ X _75_ = _75_

___ _____ _____ X _____ = _____

©2012 Sam Spencer

148

Appendix H

Recipe Calculator

_____ Number Of Preparations _____ Recipe

Volume	Ingredient	# Preparations	Total Needed		Total Needed
___ Cups _____		X _____	= _____	÷ 16 = _____	Gallons
___ Cups _____		X _____	= _____	÷ 16 = _____	Gallons
___ Cups _____		X _____	= _____	÷ 16 = _____	Gallons
___ Cups _____		X _____	= _____	÷ 16 = _____	Gallons
___ Cups _____		X _____	= _____	÷ 16 = _____	Gallons
___ Cups _____		X _____	= _____	÷ 16 = _____	Gallons
___ Tbls. _____		X _____	= _____	÷ 16 = _____	Cups
___ Tbls. _____		X _____	= _____	÷ 16 = _____	Cups
___ Tbls. _____		X _____	= _____	÷ 16 = _____	Cups
___ Tbls. _____		X _____	= _____	÷ 16 = _____	Cups
___ Tbls. _____		X _____	= _____	÷ 16 = _____	Cups
___ tsps. _____		X _____	= _____	÷ 48 = _____	Cups
___ tsps. _____		X _____	= _____	÷ 48 = _____	Cups
___ tsps. _____		X _____	= _____	÷ 48 = _____	Cups
___ tsps. _____		X _____	= _____	÷ 48 = _____	Cups

Other Ingredients:

___ _____ _____ X _____ = _____

___ _____ _____ X _____ = _____

___ _____ _____ X _____ = _____

___ _____ _____ X _____ = _____

Appendix H

Recipe Calculator

_____ Number Of Preparations _____ Recipe

Volume	Ingredient		# Preparations	Total Needed		Total Needed
___ Cups	_____	X _____	=	_____ ÷ 16 =	_____	Gallons
___ Cups	_____	X _____	=	_____ ÷ 16 =	_____	Gallons
___ Cups	_____	X _____	=	_____ ÷ 16 =	_____	Gallons
___ Cups	_____	X _____	=	_____ ÷ 16 =	_____	Gallons
___ Cups	_____	X _____	=	_____ ÷ 16 =	_____	Gallons
___ Cups	_____	X _____	=	_____ ÷ 16 =	_____	Gallons
___ Tbls.	_____	X _____	=	_____ ÷ 16 =	_____	Cups
___ Tbls.	_____	X _____	=	_____ ÷ 16 =	_____	Cups
___ Tbls.	_____	X _____	=	_____ ÷ 16 =	_____	Cups
___ Tbls.	_____	X _____	=	_____ ÷ 16 =	_____	Cups
___ Tbls.	_____	X _____	=	_____ ÷ 16 =	_____	Cups
___ tsps.	_____	X _____	=	_____ ÷ 48 =	_____	Cups
___ tsps.	_____	X _____	=	_____ ÷ 48 =	_____	Cups
___ tsps.	_____	X _____	=	_____ ÷ 48 =	_____	Cups
___ tsps.	_____	X _____	=	_____ ÷ 48 =	_____	Cups

Other Ingredients:

___ _____ _____ X _____ = _____

___ _____ _____ X _____ = _____

___ _____ _____ X _____ = _____

___ _____ _____ X _____ = _____

Appendix H

Recipe Calculator

_____ Number Of Preparations _____ Recipe

Volume	Ingredient	# Preparations	Total Needed	Total Needed
___ Cups	_____ X	_____ =	_____ ÷ 16 =	_____ Gallons
___ Cups	_____ X	_____ =	_____ ÷ 16 =	_____ Gallons
___ Cups	_____ X	_____ =	_____ ÷ 16 =	_____ Gallons
___ Cups	_____ X	_____ =	_____ ÷ 16 =	_____ Gallons
___ Cups	_____ X	_____ =	_____ ÷ 16 =	_____ Gallons
___ Cups	_____ X	_____ =	_____ ÷ 16 =	_____ Gallons
___ Tbls.	_____ X	_____ =	_____ ÷ 16 =	_____ Cups
___ Tbls.	_____ X	_____ =	_____ ÷ 16 =	_____ Cups
___ Tbls.	_____ X	_____ =	_____ ÷ 16 =	_____ Cups
___ Tbls.	_____ X	_____ =	_____ ÷ 16 =	_____ Cups
___ Tbls.	_____ X	_____ =	_____ ÷ 16 =	_____ Cups
___ tsps.	_____ X	_____ =	_____ ÷ 48 =	_____ Cups
___ tsps.	_____ X	_____ =	_____ ÷ 48 =	_____ Cups
___ tsps.	_____ X	_____ =	_____ ÷ 48 =	_____ Cups
___ tsps.	_____ X	_____ =	_____ ÷ 48 =	_____ Cups

Other Ingredients:

___ _____ _____ X _____ = _____

___ _____ _____ X _____ = _____

___ _____ _____ X _____ = _____

___ _____ _____ X _____ = _____

Appendix H

Recipe Calculator

_____ Number Of Preparations _____ Recipe

Volume	Ingredient		# Preparations	Total Needed		Total Needed
___ Cups	_____	X	_____	= _____	÷ 16 = _____	Gallons
___ Cups	_____	X	_____	= _____	÷ 16 = _____	Gallons
___ Cups	_____	X	_____	= _____	÷ 16 = _____	Gallons
___ Cups	_____	X	_____	= _____	÷ 16 = _____	Gallons
___ Cups	_____	X	_____	= _____	÷ 16 = _____	Gallons
___ Cups	_____	X	_____	= _____	÷ 16 = _____	Gallons
___ Tbls.	_____	X	_____	= _____	÷ 16 = _____	Cups
___ Tbls.	_____	X	_____	= _____	÷ 16 = _____	Cups
___ Tbls.	_____	X	_____	= _____	÷ 16 = _____	Cups
___ Tbls.	_____	X	_____	= _____	÷ 16 = _____	Cups
___ Tbls.	_____	X	_____	= _____	÷ 16 = _____	Cups
___ tsps.	_____	X	_____	= _____	÷ 48 = _____	Cups
___ tsps.	_____	X	_____	= _____	÷ 48 = _____	Cups
___ tsps.	_____	X	_____	= _____	÷ 48 = _____	Cups
___ tsps.	_____	X	_____	= _____	÷ 48 = _____	Cups

Other Ingredients:

___ _____ _____ X _____ = _____

___ _____ _____ X _____ = _____

___ _____ _____ X _____ = _____

___ _____ _____ X _____ = _____

Appendix H

Recipe Calculator

_____ Number Of Preparations _____ Recipe

Volume	Ingredient	# Preparations	Total Needed		Total Needed
___ Cups	_____ X	_____ =	_____ ÷ 16 =	_____	Gallons
___ Cups	_____ X	_____ =	_____ ÷ 16 =	_____	Gallons
___ Cups	_____ X	_____ =	_____ ÷ 16 =	_____	Gallons
___ Cups	_____ X	_____ =	_____ ÷ 16 =	_____	Gallons
___ Cups	_____ X	_____ =	_____ ÷ 16 =	_____	Gallons
___ Cups	_____ X	_____ =	_____ ÷ 16 =	_____	Gallons
___ Tbls.	_____ X	_____ =	_____ ÷ 16 =	_____	Cups
___ Tbls.	_____ X	_____ =	÷ 16 =	_____	Cups
___ Tbls.	_____ X	_____ =	_____ ÷ 16 =	_____	Cups
___ Tbls.	_____ X	_____ =	_____ ÷ 16 =	_____	Cups
___ Tbls.	_____ X	_____ =	_____ ÷ 16 =	_____	Cups
___ tsps.	_____ X	_____ =	_____ ÷ 48 =	_____	Cups
___ tsps.	_____ X	_____ =	_____ ÷ 48 =	_____	Cups
___ tsps.	_____ X	_____ =	_____ ÷ 48 =	_____	Cups
___ tsps.	_____ X	_____ =	_____ ÷ 48 =	_____	Cups

Other Ingredients:

___ _____ _____ X _____ = _____

___ _____ _____ X _____ = _____

___ _____ _____ X _____ = _____

___ _____ _____ X _____ = _____

Appendix H

Recipe Calculator

_____ Number Of Preparations _____ Recipe

Volume	Ingredient	# Preparations	Total Needed		Total Needed
___ Cups	_____	X _____	= _____	÷ 16 =	_____ Gallons
___ Cups	_____	X _____	= _____	÷ 16 =	_____ Gallons
___ Cups	_____	X _____	= _____	÷ 16 =	_____ Gallons
___ Cups	_____	X _____	= _____	÷ 16 =	_____ Gallons
___ Cups	_____	X _____	= _____	÷ 16 =	_____ Gallons
___ Cups	_____	X _____	= _____	÷ 16 =	_____ Gallons
___ Tbls.	_____	X _____	= _____	÷ 16 =	_____ Cups
___ Tbls.	_____	X _____	= _____	÷ 16 =	_____ Cups
___ Tbls.	_____	X _____	= _____	÷ 16 =	_____ Cups
___ Tbls.	_____	X _____	= _____	÷ 16 =	_____ Cups
___ Tbls.	_____	X _____	= _____	÷ 16 =	_____ Cups
___ tsps.	_____	X _____	= _____	÷ 48 =	_____ Cups
___ tsps.	_____	X _____	= _____	÷ 48 =	_____ Cups
___ tsps.	_____	X _____	= _____	÷ 48 =	_____ Cups
___ tsps.	_____	X _____	= _____	÷ 48 =	_____ Cups

Other Ingredients:

___ _____ _____ X _____ = _____

___ _____ _____ X _____ = _____

___ _____ _____ X _____ = _____

___ _____ _____ X _____ = _____

Appendix H

Recipe Calculator

_____ Number Of Preparations _____ Recipe

Volume	Ingredient		# Preparations	Total Needed		Total Needed
___ Cups	_____	X _____	= _____	÷ 16 =	_____	Gallons
___ Cups	_____	X _____	= _____	÷ 16 =	_____	Gallons
___ Cups	_____	X _____	= _____	÷ 16 =	_____	Gallons
___ Cups	_____	X _____	= _____	÷ 16 =	_____	Gallons
___ Cups	_____	X _____	= _____	÷ 16 =	_____	Gallons
___ Cups	_____	X _____	= _____	÷ 16 =	_____	Gallons
___ Tbls.	_____	X _____	= _____	÷ 16 =	_____	Cups
___ Tbls.		X _____	= _____	÷ 16 =	_____	Cups
___ Tbls.	_____	X _____	= _____	÷ 16 =	_____	Cups
___ Tbls.	_____	X _____	= _____	÷ 16 =	_____	Cups
___ Tbls.	_____	X _____	= _____	÷ 16 =	_____	Cups
___ tsps.	_____	X _____	= _____	÷ 48 =	_____	Cups
___ tsps.	_____	X _____	= _____	÷ 48 =	_____	Cups
___ tsps.	_____	X _____	= _____	÷ 48 =	_____	Cups
___ tsps.	_____	X _____	= _____	÷ 48 =	_____	Cups

Other Ingredients:

___ _____	_____	X _____	= _____
___ _____	_____	X _____	= _____
___ _____	_____	X _____	= _____
___ _____	_____	X _____	= _____

Appendix H

Recipe Calculator

_____ Number Of Preparations _____ Recipe

Volume	Ingredient		# Preparations	Total Needed		Total Needed	
___ Cups	_____	X	_____	= _____	÷ 16 =	_____	Gallons
___ Cups	_____	X	_____	= _____	÷ 16 =	_____	Gallons
___ Cups	_____	X	_____	= _____	÷ 16 =	_____	Gallons
___ Cups	_____	X	_____	= _____	÷ 16 =	_____	Gallons
___ Cups	_____	X	_____	= _____	÷ 16 =	_____	Gallons
___ Cups	_____	X	_____	= _____	÷ 16 =	_____	Gallons
___ Tbls.	_____	X	_____	= _____	÷ 16 =	_____	Cups
___ Tbls.	_____	X	_____	= _____	÷ 16 =	_____	Cups
___ Tbls.	_____	X	_____	= _____	÷ 16 =	_____	Cups
___ Tbls.	_____	X	_____	= _____	÷ 16 =	_____	Cups
___ Tbls.	_____	X	_____	= _____	÷ 16 =	_____	Cups
___ tsps.	_____	X	_____	= _____	÷ 48 =	_____	Cups
___ tsps.	_____	X	_____	= _____	÷ 48 =	_____	Cups
___ tsps.	_____	X	_____	= _____	÷ 48 =	_____	Cups
___ tsps.	_____	X	_____	= _____	÷ 48 =	_____	Cups

Other Ingredients:

___ _____ _____ X _____ = _____

___ _____ _____ X _____ = _____

___ _____ _____ X _____ = _____

___ _____ _____ X _____ = _____

Appendix H

Recipe Calculator

_____ Number Of Preparations _____ Recipe

Volume	Ingredient	# Preparations	Total Needed		Total Needed
___ Cups	_____	X _____	= _____	÷ 16 = _____	Gallons
___ Cups	_____	X _____	= _____	÷ 16 = _____	Gallons
___ Cups	_____	X _____	= _____	÷ 16 = _____	Gallons
___ Cups	_____	X _____	= _____	÷ 16 = _____	Gallons
___ Cups	_____	X _____	= _____	÷ 16 = _____	Gallons
___ Cups	_____	X _____	= _____	÷ 16 = _____	Gallons
___ Tbls.	_____	X _____	= _____	÷ 16 = _____	Cups
___ Tbls.	_____	X _____	= _____	÷ 16 = _____	Cups
___ Tbls.	_____	X _____	= _____	÷ 16 = _____	Cups
___ Tbls.	_____	X _____	= _____	÷ 16 = _____	Cups
___ Tbls.	_____	X _____	= _____	÷ 16 = _____	Cups
___ tsps.	_____	X _____	= _____	÷ 48 = _____	Cups
___ tsps.	_____	X _____	= _____	÷ 48 = _____	Cups
___ tsps.	_____	X _____	= _____	÷ 48 = _____	Cups
___ tsps.	_____	X _____	= _____	÷ 48 = _____	Cups

Other Ingredients:

___ _____ _____ X _____ = _____

___ _____ _____ X _____ = _____

___ _____ _____ X _____ = _____

___ _____ _____ X _____ = _____

www.ingramcontent.com/pod-product-compliance
Lightning Source LLC
Chambersburg PA
CBHW050128280326
41933CB00010B/1286